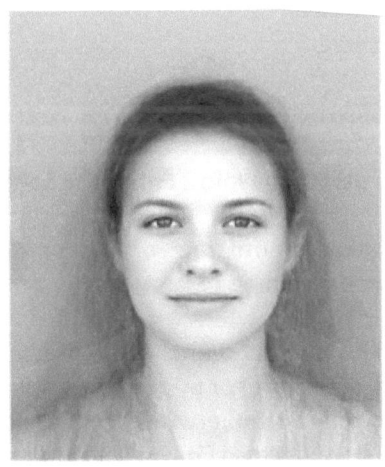

Identity Management on a Shoestring
Architectural Lessons from a Real-World Implementation

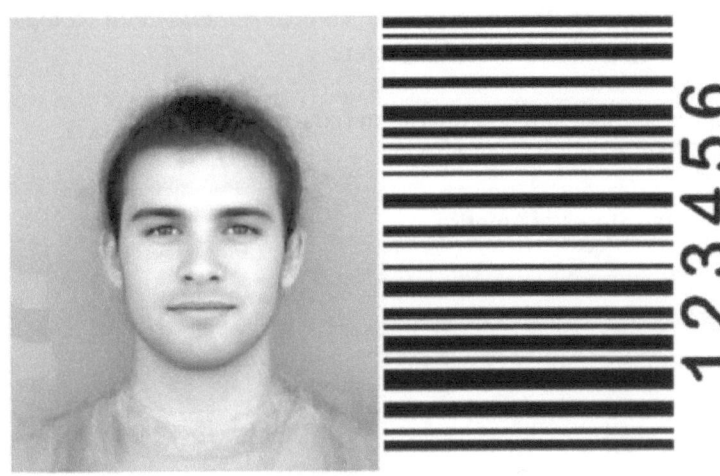

a book by

Ganesh Prasad & Umesh Rajbhandari

InfoQ
ENTERPRISE SOFTWARE
DEVELOPMENT SERIES

© 2010 C4Media Inc.
All rights reserved.

C4Media, Publisher of InfoQ.com.

This book is part of the InfoQ Enterprise Software Development series of books.

For information or ordering of this or other InfoQ books, please contact books@c4media.com.

No part of this publication may be reproduced, stored in a retrieval system or transmitted in any form or by any means, electronic, mechanical, photocopying, recoding, scanning or otherwise except as permitted under Sections 107 or 108 of the 1976 United States Copyright Act, without the prior written permission of the Publisher.

Designations used by companies to distinguish their products are often claimed as trademarks. In all instances where C4Media Inc. is aware of a claim, the product names appear in Initial Capital or ALL CAPITAL LETTERS. Readers, however, should contact the appropriate companies for more complete information regarding trademarks and registration.

Library of Congress Cataloguing-in-Publication Data:
ISBN: 978-1-105-06556-9

Printed in the United States of America

Acknowledgements

Our grateful thanks to Edward Chin, without whose unstinting support and organisational *nous* our bold experiment would never have got off the ground, much less achieved the penetration it has today.

Intended Audience

This document is aimed at Security and IT practitioners (especially architects) in end-user organisations who are responsible for implementing an enterprise-wide Identity and Access Management (IAM) system. It is neither a conceptual treatment of Identity (for which we would refer the reader to Kim Cameron's excellent work on the Laws of Identity) nor a detailed technical manual on a particular product. It describes a pragmatic and cost-effective architectural approach to implementing IAM within an organisation, based on the experience of the authors.

Starting in early 2009, we built an IAM system for a large and established Australian financial services company, using a rather unconventional approach. While the system has not yet reached its envisioned target state, we have had significant success so far, and we believe our experience carries valuable lessons for others considering a similar journey. Identity Management as an applied practice does not enjoy a rich knowledge base in the public domain, so we are pleased to contribute our experience herewith. Most of what we describe here is from what we have already implemented and proven. Some of it refers to planned designs to meet forthcoming requirements, and some of it reflects (with the benefit of hindsight) the way we *wish* our solution had been designed! We have distilled these learnings into an architectural approach we call LIMA[1].

Our background and experience are largely with Java-based technologies, so Java shops would probably be best positioned to benefit from our suggestions, but we are sure these general principles can be suitably adapted to other technology platforms.

As with any piece of unsolicited advice, the usual caveats apply. No guarantees or warranties are provided or implied. The reader is expected to apply common sense and sound design judgement when developing a solution based on this approach.

---

1   Low-cost/Lightweight/Loosely-coupled Identity Management Architecture

Cover Illustration

The male and female faces on the cover are South African photographer Mike Mike's "average" faces of Sydney, morphed from a hundred photographs of real people in the suburb of Bondi, Sydney. From the standpoint of identity, they are as non-specific as a fingerprint or barcode are specific, and we hope that provides you with something philosophical to mull over with your evening glass of wine.

Contents

- ACKNOWLEDGEMENTS III
- INTENDED AUDIENCE III
- COVER ILLUSTRATION IV
- CONTENTS V

LIMA AT A GLANCE 1
- LESSONS LEARNT FROM TRADITIONAL IAM IMPLEMENTATIONS 1

INTRODUCTION 7

THE MODERN ENTERPRISE – A REALITY CHECK 10
- SO YOU THINK YOU'RE GOING TO CHANGE THE WORLD 10
- WHO'S YOUR SUGAR DADDY? FUNDING MODELS THAT WORK 12
- FIRST THINGS FIRST – OBJECTIVES OF IDENTITY AND ACCESS MANAGEMENT 14
- THE TROUBLE WITH BRAND-NAME PRODUCTS 16
- MISCONCEPTIONS ABOUT SECURITY 20
- AUDITORS, SECURITY AND WORDS OF WISDOM 22

INTRODUCING LIMA – A DIFFERENT ARCHITECTURE FOR IAM 24
- LOOSE COUPLING – A FIRM FOUNDATION FOR IAM 24
- SNEAK PREVIEW – WHAT A LIMA IMPLEMENTATION LOOKS LIKE 29

ACCESS MANAGEMENT, LIMA-STYLE 34
- ACCESS MANAGEMENT CONCEPTS 34
- HOW SINGLE SIGN-ON WORKS 40
- THE BEST THINGS IN LIFE (AND IN IAM) ARE FREE 42
- CENTRAL AUTHENTICATION SERVICE AND THE CAS PROTOCOL 44
- SHIBBOLETH'S FEDERATED IDENTITY MODEL 47
- CAS SERVER CONFIGURATION AND THE "TWO-LAYER PROTOCOL ARCHITECTURE" 50
- ENHANCING ACCESS MANAGEMENT FUNCTIONALITY INCREMENTALLY 53
  - *Extension Case Study 1: LAN SSO Integration with SPNEGO* 53
  - *Extension Case Study 2: Two-Factor Authentication with SMS One-Time Tokens* 59
  - *Extension Case Study 3: Federated Identity with SAML Tokens* 62
- LIMITS TO THE TWO-LAYER PROTOCOL ARCHITECTURE 66
- MISCELLANEOUS TOPICS IN ACCESS MANAGEMENT 70
  - *Protecting Non-Web Applications* 70
  - *Implementing "Single Sign-Out"* 72
  - *IAM and Cloud Computing* 74

What Do We Do with Active Directory? 76
Tailoring Coarse-Grained Access Control 78
Using CAS to Centralise Enforcement of Authorisation Rules 80
Using a Reverse-Proxy Device as a Common Interceptor 82
Access Management for "Portal" Applications 84

IDENTITY MANAGEMENT, LIMA-STYLE 86

IDENTITY MANAGEMENT CONCEPTS 86
SEPARATING CHURCH AND STATE – THE ROLES OF DIRECTORY AND DATABASE 87
DESIGNING THE IAM DIRECTORY 89
USER UUID – THE ONE RING TO RULE THEM ALL 93
DECOUPLING AUTHENTICATION, COARSE-GRAINED AND FINE-GRAINED AUTHORISATION REALMS 94
PERSON UUID – THE ULTIMATE IDENTITY REFERENCE 96
DATA REPLICATION AND MASTER DATA MANAGEMENT 98
DESIGNING THE IAM DATABASE 99
REST EASY WITH REST SERVICES 106
IAM REST SERVICE INTERFACE AT A GLANCE 108
AUTOMATED USER PROVISIONING – INVOCATION OF REST SERVICES 109
USER ADMINISTRATION 112
IAM, PROTECT THYSELF 117
PROVISIONING USERS TO DOWNSTREAM SYSTEMS 119
DESIGNING USER PROVISIONING MESSAGES 122

IMPLEMENTING LIMA 127

TRANSITIONING TO THE TARGET STATE 128
Harmonising data 128
Managing SSO realms 128
Manual provisioning 130
THE BAU OF IAM – A "COOKIE-CUTTER" IMPLEMENTATION 131
Development tasks 131
Provisioning tasks 132

CONCLUSION 133

APPENDIX A – TYPICAL SECURITY REQUIREMENTS FROM AN IAM SYSTEM 134
APPENDIX C – SPECIAL CASE EXAMPLE 1 (MULTIPLEXING USER IDS) 137
APPENDIX D – SPECIAL CASE EXAMPLE 2 (RESETTING LAN PASSWORDS) 140
APPENDIX E – A SAMPLE PHASED ROLL-OUT PLAN 142
ABOUT THE AUTHORS 143

LIMA at a Glance

Lessons learnt from traditional IAM implementations

This document is about a radically different approach to Identity and Access Management (IAM) called LIMA (Lightweight/Low-cost/Loosely-coupled Identity Management Architecture). It is based on the lessons learnt from traditional IAM initiatives, and recognises that:

1. **IAM isn't monolithic.** Identity and Access Management has two distinct domains that require to be approached differently,

   - Access Management (which is a real-time function controlling user authentication and authorisation at the time users attempt to access resources), and
   - Identity Management (which is a somewhat less real-time back-end function dealing with user provisioning and related data management, and the audit function)

2. **Off-the-shelf IAM products are more trouble than they're worth.** Attempting to implement IAM using a single monolithic Identity Management product often doesn't work in practice, for technical as well as for financial reasons. The product's tightly coupled components create logistical complexity, and "Big Bang" funding is generally required, which either taxes the enterprise budget or the first business project. Loose coupling is a much better architectural approach that imposes only incremental costs, is affordable by projects and eases the integration of future components.

3. **There are no security shortcuts from any particular approach.** Identity Management almost always requires tailoring or customisation to suit an individual organisation's requirements, which from a security perspective necessitates an end-to-end audit of all processes prior to implementation. Prior security certifications don't mean much when processes are customised, which negates the basic security argument in favour of packaged products over loosely-coupled components from multiple sources.

4. **Commercial Access Management solutions are a waste of money.** Access Management is highly commoditised today and can be readily implemented using cost-effective and certified Open Source components, all without

compromising the key cryptographic techniques used for user authentication. The integration of these components to Identity Management is through *data*.

5. **Data design is a key part of loose coupling**. A core reality to work with (rather than work against) is that existing identifiers within systems are local, but User Identity needs to be global. The use of a meaning-free and globally unique yet federated identifier for each unique user entity is a simple approach that facilitates integration across distributed systems through *association* with local identifiers. This association can be maintained in either a centralised or decentralised manner as required.

6. **Authorisation data is best separated into coarse-grained and fine-grained access rules**. Business applications generally implement fine-grained access control logic as an inherent part of their business logic and this cannot usually be factored out, especially with COTS (Commercial off-the-shelf) applications. Only coarse-grained access rules should be managed in IAM. The association between the global, meaning-free identifier and the local identifiers should be leveraged to coordinate the uniform enforcement of access control logic.

7. **User provisioning processes can be much simpler than you think**. The complex workflow supported in many Identity Management products is overkill. Segregation of duties can be ensured without "workflow". With appropriate data design, it is also easy to keep multiple user data stores mutually consistent without complex synchronisation or replication.

8. **You can't avoid bespoke development**. User Provisioning and Audit functions are not as generic as they may seem. An organisation's requirements may have their own unique quirks that need to be addressed. Fortunately, these functions are quite easy to build as bespoke modules, provided some general security principles are followed and the system is audited before implementation.

The rest of this document will expand on these insights and provide practical guidelines for an implementation. The following overview diagrams may help set the stage for the detailed description that follows.

The core problem – Being unable to correlate related data

Multiple systems store user data; each holds data about a subset of users, and the data itself is a subset of a user's attributes.

Each system has a locally unique "primary key", which is some unique identifier for a user within that data store. The primary key is never null (blank) and it always identifies a single user (no duplicates). The primary keys in different systems are independent and not necessarily consistent.

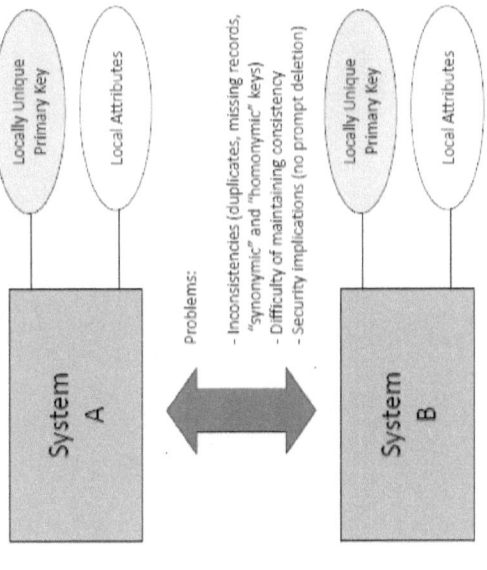

Fig 1: The problem of "Fractured Identity"

Tiptoeing around sleeping dragons – "Harmonising" works better than "Unifying"

Introduce a new and globally unique *candidate* key to harmonise records across systems rather than try and force consistency of local primary keys.

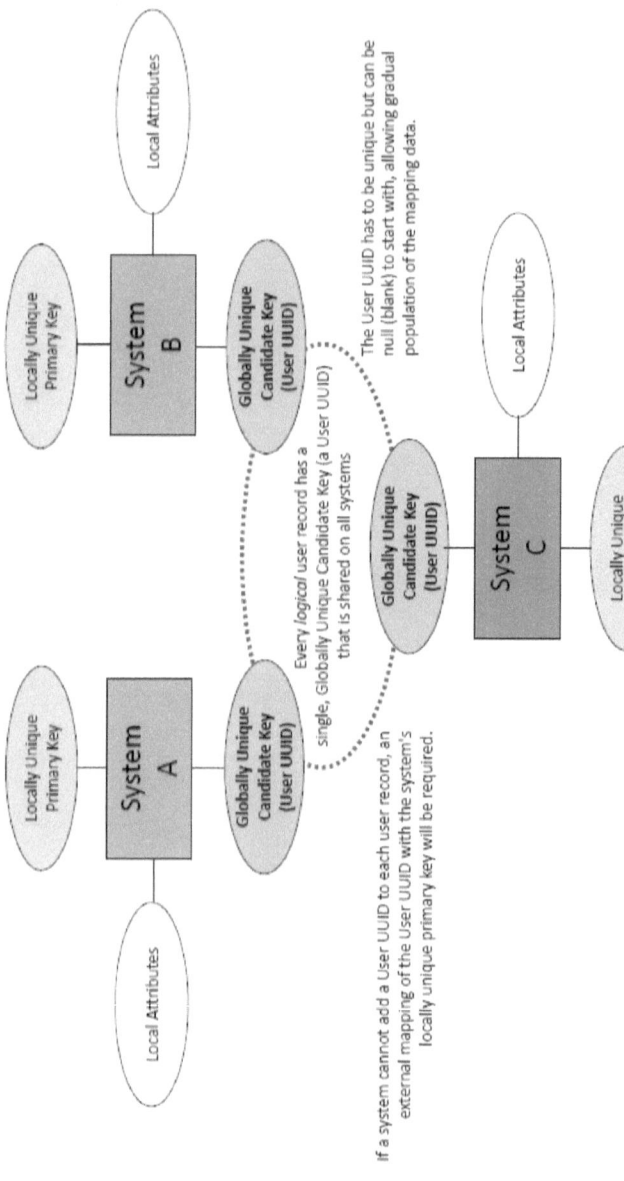

Fig 2: Integrating identity, non-intrusively

Identity Management on a Shoestring

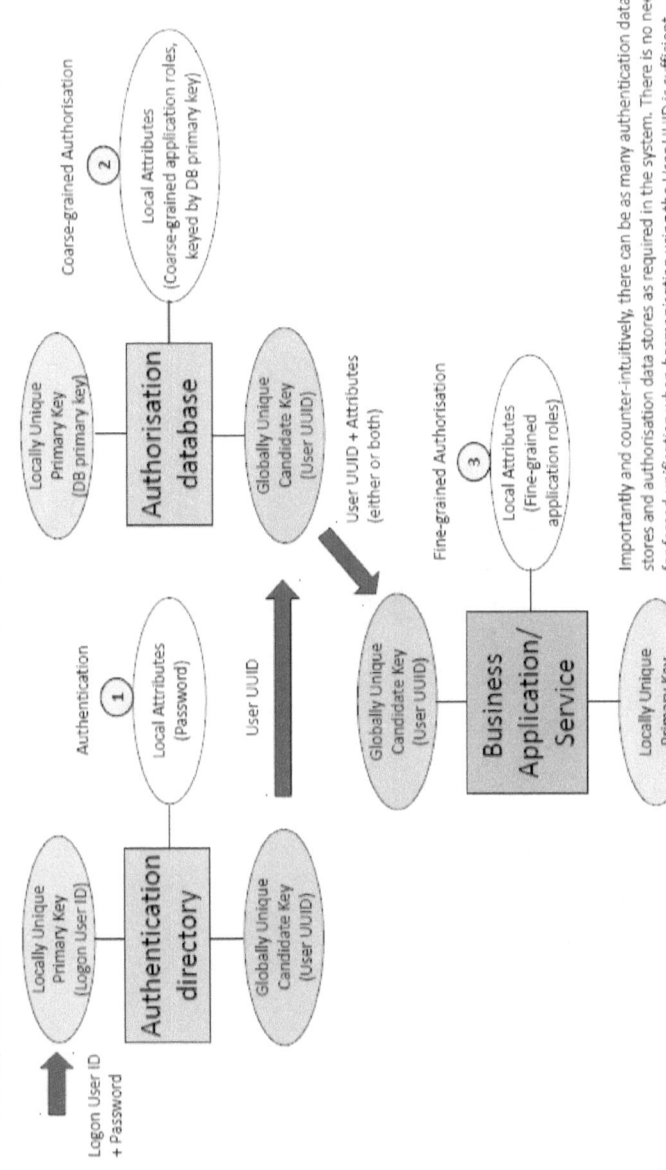

Fig 3: *How Authentication and Authorisation should work*

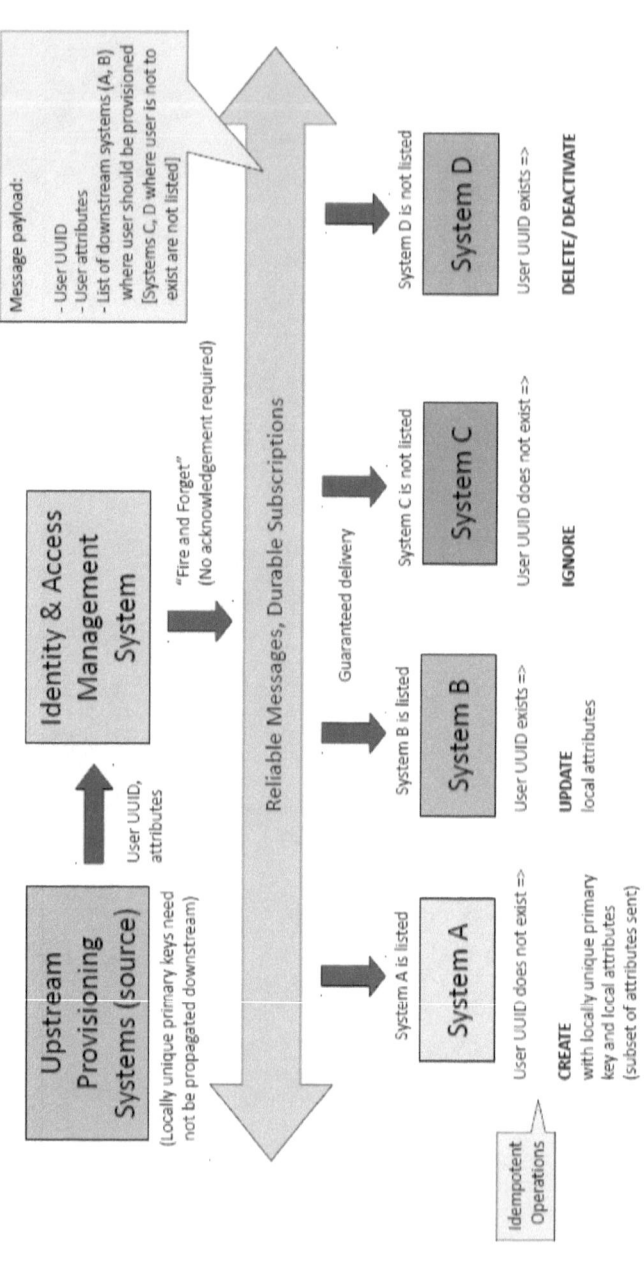

Fig 4: How User Provisioning should work

Introduction

When you read the literature or talk to the experts, you may come away with the impression that IAM (Identity and Access Management)[2] is a huge and complex domain.

In our experience, that's just not true. Like SOA (Service-Oriented Architecture), IAM may not be easy. But it is simple[3]. Here is essentially the value that Identity and Access Management adds to your business functions:

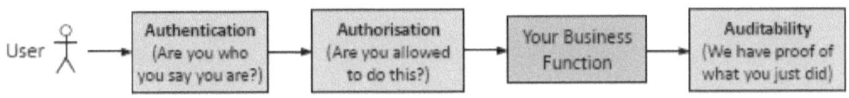

Fig 5: IAM Functions

Once you understand some simple principles, you can very quickly see what needs to be done to enable this, and (with some guidance) even how to do it. But ah, actually doing it is the killer! It takes political will, a battering ram and very thick skin to be able to steer an organisation to a simpler place, from which point onwards (funnily enough), everything becomes easy as well.

What actually happens in practice? Faced with a task that is simple but not easy, organisations generally do the most expedient thing. They go out and buy a product. Because buying a product is easy.

A couple of years and oodles of dollars later, organisations then wonder why the promised goodies failed to materialise. The honest ones organise a court-martial and a firing squad. The dishonest ones (the majority) tend to declare victory regardless. In one egregious case, an organisation we know spent tens of millions of dollars on IAM without even achieving Single Sign-On capability! *And no heads rolled.*

It doesn't have to be that way. This document is meant to cut a lot of time, expense and suffering out of your IAM journey. It won't give you the political will or the thick skin, of course. That's your stuff. What it will do is show you how simple IAM really

---

[2] To be exact, Identity Management includes Access Management, so we will refer to the combined capability as IAM (Identity and Access Management) throughout this document, although the common industry term seems to be just Identity Management.

[3] By way of analogy, "Don't tell lies" is a simple principle, but not an easy one to follow!

is. The architecture we describe here can quite literally save you millions of dollars, if you can just get your organisation around to implementing it.

The following diagram shows you the basic functions of IAM at a glance[4], and the subsequent sections will gradually provide more detail, so as to ease you into this really simple way of approaching IAM. (Confidentiality agreements with employers past and present prevent us from sharing specific design details and code from our experience, but principles, patterns and tips are as free as the air we breathe, and as precious.)

We hope our experience will benefit you in your own journey. Good luck!

---

[4] Also see Appendix B for a more formal model of Identity and Access Management.

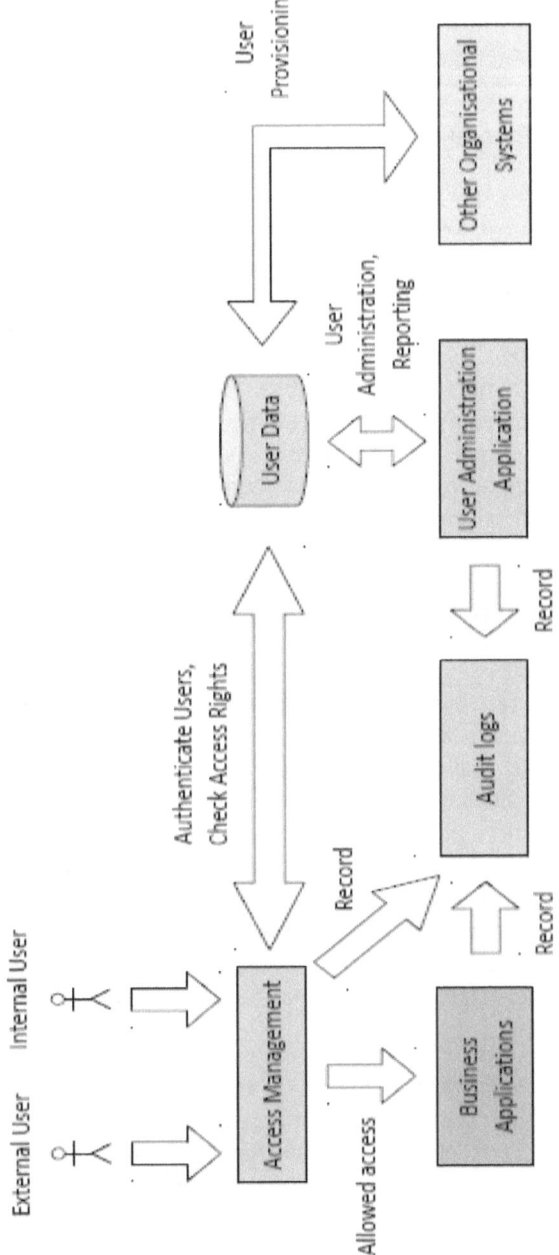

Fig 6: IAM at a glance

The Modern Enterprise – A Reality Check

So You Think You're Going to Change the World

If you're reading this document, it's probably because you're an enthusiastic and idealistic change agent who wants to shake up their organisation with a simpler, faster and cheaper model. That's great, but we're painfully aware that even our simple and cost-effective approach may not work for you, because your organisation may just not have the right culture to accept solutions like this.

What makes it really hard to implement an IAM system isn't the technology. You would be half right if you thought it was data. Yes, cleaning and reorganising huge volumes of legacy data are moderately hard tasks, but they're not exactly insurmountable. What can stop your IAM initiative in its tracks is that elusive beast known as organisational culture.

Here are some killer characteristics we have identified. If you perceive a scarily close resemblance to your own organisation, stop reading this paper right now. It will only frustrate you needlessly.

Brand-Name Idolatry: Some organisations will only buy "reputed" products from big brand-name vendors. We've heard all the arguments about risk that are raised in such organisations, and our cynical observation is that this is more about political risk to decision-makers (i.e., "Nobody ever got fired for buying IBM") than any real risk to the organisation. In our experience, the brand-name path involves plenty of effort and expense, and a rather low probability of success[5], for reasons we cover in a later section. If this is your organisation (especially if your security auditors put their faith in products rather than in adherence to principles), you should probably fall in line and console yourself with the thought that they deserve to waste their money anyway. Cost-effective solutions take a back seat to political survival at such organisations.

Hostile Fiefdoms: People and systems need to play ball, at least to some extent. If there are areas in your organisation that require to be brought under the ambit of IAM, but they refuse to change the way they work and are powerful enough to resist pressure to do so, then you should probably pick an easier project. Likewise, when powerful persons or groups decide for whatever reason to oppose your

---

[5] Projects that greatly exceed budgets should also be counted as failures.

approach, either overtly or in a passive-aggressive manner, you will need powerful backers of your own, or else failure is virtually guaranteed.

Zombies: Sometimes, past (misguided) attempts at implementing an IAM system create legacy components that continue to limp on in a twilight zone. You will find it extra hard to convince people of the superiority of your approach if it means undoing what has been done earlier. That would be an admission of failure – always a no-no from a political perspective! In addition, management sometimes doesn't seem to understand the term "sunk costs" and may keep throwing good money after bad. It will be hard to turn this Titanic around once it has set its heart on reaching that iceberg, so it would be prudent to grab a lifeboat and abandon ship.

If you've made it this far, it probably augurs well for your plans, so let's proceed.

Notice that we have not listed "Funding Model" as a problem for our approach. Why not?

Who's Your Sugar Daddy? Funding Models That Work

It's true that inadequate attention to funding can kill many prospective IAM initiatives. That's because most organisations have a "first project pays" policy even for the creation of shared enterprise utilities. Integration of applications with big brand-name Identity Management products typically involves huge upfront costs (licensing as well as initial effort), and the very first roll-out tends to be too expensive for any single business project to bear. That's why many IAM initiatives fail at the starting line. Sometimes, a one-time injection of enterprise funding gets such projects over the starting line, but IAM needs to cover all major applications to be effective, and from a logistical angle, this is necessarily a multi-year roll-out exercise. Without a long-term vision and a phased multi-year budget, subsequent roll-outs tend to go unfunded or place an onerous burden on business projects. Accordingly, these initiatives then either peter out or impose unforeseen ongoing costs to the organisation.

The approach we describe here has been specifically designed to work around these funding constraints, because this is a problem we ourselves faced and had to tackle. It is therefore lightweight and can be rolled out piecemeal.

Every component is simple, minimal and relatively inexpensive. Using this approach, you can roll out your IAM system over a multi-year period without incurring the full cost up front. The loosely-coupled nature of the solution also makes it feasible to implement just the parts each project needs. There are no artificial dependencies that force the deployment of unnecessary components at extra cost. Every project can independently justify the business case for funding that part of the IAM solution that it requires, because the returns are also immediate and incremental[6].

We recommend that you plan and organise these incremental roll-outs into a coherent multi-year roadmap that leads to your desired target state through a series of intermediate stages. Align these stages with the specific capabilities that business projects are looking for, and piggyback off those projects for funding[7]. You may also find that each step on this journey costs less than the previous one because you leverage off the assets that have already been created and you need

---

[6] The next section lists the major benefits from IAM that can be used to build up a business case.

[7] Appendix E provides a sample roadmap that you can tailor to your organisation's context.

smaller and smaller *additional* capability. Eventually, rolling out IAM to a new application becomes a "cookie-cutter" operation[8].

Enterprise funding is a bonus with this approach, but not essential. Enterprise funding could be seen more as a lubricant, paying for tasks and components that the more finicky business projects may baulk at paying for. Such funding would typically be small and infrequent, and definitely not comparable to the Big Bang roll-outs of enterprise IAM initiatives. Squirrel away a small slush fund that can enable such activities :-).

---

[8] One of the last sections in this document lists out the typical tasks involved when you get to the "cookie-cutter" roll-out stage.

First Things First – Objectives of Identity and Access Management

Before we get all excited and dive into the details of our solution, it's critically important to understand why you may need an IAM solution in the first place. Far too many organisations jump into the product procurement activity without a clear understanding of what they intend to achieve from implementing IAM. The term "Single Sign-On" is often used synonymously with IAM, but while this is readily understandable to end-users, it's only a nice-to-have in the larger scheme of things, and the business case simply doesn't stack up when that is the only planned benefit. Fortunately, it so happens that IAM is about a lot more than Single Sign-On.

Put simply, the drivers for IAM usually revolve around three considerations – Risk & Compliance, Cost Reduction and Convenience. Typical objectives, in descending order of importance, are:

I Risk & Compliance

1. To secure information assets and restrict their access only to legitimate users through authentication and authorisation, and to protect against business, legal and reputation risk arising from inappropriate access
2. To ensure compliance with enterprise security policy across all applications and information assets (e.g., through password policies, role-based access control, etc.) and meet internal and external audit requirements
3. To ensure accountability through role-based access, approval processes and audit trails of relevant user activity (e.g., logins, failed logins, application accesses, etc.)

II Cost Reduction

1. To reduce the effort (i.e., support staff headcount) involved in manual provisioning, de-provisioning and user management, through automation and self-service, especially with increasing volumes
2. To eliminate or reduce the cost of errors, delays and inefficiencies arising from manual processes and other elements of waste (e.g., orphan accounts, unused storage, etc.)

III Convenience

1. To provide a Single Sign-On (SSO) environment to users (eliminating the need to remember multiple sets of authentication credentials)

2. To expedite operations through self-service features (e.g., password reset/forgotten password, delegated administration, etc.)

Some organisations also hope to achieve a "Single View of Customer" through implementing IAM, which allows them to understand customer behaviour better and to enable up-selling and cross-selling of products.

If you want to make out a business case for an IAM system, you will need to provide some variant of the above list of benefits from the proposed exercise. Hopefully, the approach we outline in the following pages will also give you enough input to help you quantify the cost of the solution, so you can see if your business case stands up. We think it will.

The Trouble with Brand-Name Products

This is probably one of the most controversial topics in this document, which is why we have devoted a fair bit of effort to discussing it. We have arrived at our architectural approach after exhausting the alternatives, so we are very familiar with the pros and cons in this debate.

If your organisation is like most others, then the first thing you would do after determining that you need an IAM system is to look for a good off-the-shelf product. Many organisations have a practice of consulting the Gartner Magic Quadrant^{TM} or Forrester Wave^{TM} to identify the top players in the relevant market segment, then they issue RFPs (Requests for Proposal) to them, evaluate the responses, create short-lists, organise vendor presentations and Proofs of Concept, then after conducting commercial due diligence and negotiations, settle on a product and set about planning an implementation.

When organisations apply this typically "corporate" approach to sourcing an IAM solution, they usually overlook six 'C's, - problems that are common to all their candidate alternatives:

- Conceptual Subtlety
- Centralised Model of Design
- Commoditised Functionality
- Complexity of Features
- Custom Requirements
- Closed Interfaces

Conceptual Subtlety: Human nature has a bias towards the tangible. People expect the heavy lifting in an IAM ecosystem to be performed by components that they can see and touch, so to speak. A suggestion that effective integration can be achieved through appropriate data and protocol design is often unconvincing. Techniques like the use of open protocols, meaning-free and universal identifiers, master data management principles, idempotent messages, one-way notifications instead of synchronous service calls, etc., seem somewhat anticlimactic compared to "a product that does everything". Yet it is precisely these understated and unobtrusive elements of design that are the most effective. The judicious use of these techniques reduces the need for dedicated products, which may be all the more reason that IAM products don't emphasise them!

Centralised Model of Design: IAM products are in a sense victims of their own hype. A prestigious (and expensive) IAM product is expected to comprehensively manage user data by itself, because its purchase cannot otherwise be justified. Such an expectation places an onerous burden on any single application, because by its very nature, an enterprise has many different applications, many of them standalone, off-the-shelf commercial products with their own user databases, role definitions and fine-grained access control rules. If a centralised product has to manage all of this detailed and dispersed data, it will lead to two practical, logistical problems.

One, the IAM user repository will become overpopulated and excessively complicated in structure, because it has to store the fine-grained roles and access control rules of every application in the enterprise, along with the mappings of users to all those roles.

Two, since it will in most cases be impossible to remove the fine-grained access control logic from each individual application, some sort of replication, often two-way, will need to be set up to keep the IAM repository and the individual application databases in sync. What seems at first to be a simple and elegant model of centralisation is in fact operationally cumbersome and error-prone.

A model where the IAM product only manages coarse-grained roles and access control rules, and leaves fine-grained ones to each individual application, will work better in practice. However, it will seem wasteful to perform user management in multiple places, and the value of purchasing an IAM product will be questioned. "We've paid a lot of money for this product. We should use it to the maximum," will be the inevitable argument. It is very hard for common sense to prevail unless expectations are managed from the start. The vendors are mostly to blame for raising expectations in the pre-sales period which their products cannot realistically meet in a diverse ecosystem.

Commoditised Functionality: Quite frankly, the Access Management aspect of IAM is a thoroughly commoditised capability today. You can source solutions from a competitive market that includes some very capable Open Source implementations, so you don't have to pay the premiums that the market-leading vendors charge for it. You may be surprised to hear that many vendor products are priced on a per-transaction (based on the number of "hits" on a website) or per-user basis. The vendors make more money as your volumes increase, but the same capability can be sourced without having to pay such a rent, if you know where to look.

Complexity of Features: Some functions and data structures seem common to most organisations, but the generic implementations provided by major IAM products tend to be a superset of required capabilities that is more complex than warranted for any single organisation's needs. One reputed product we evaluated boasted *five* different administrator roles, which could confuse most administrators at any organisation. As another example, many IAM products boast sophisticated workflow capabilities, yet auditors only require a two-step request/authorise process to enforce the "segregation of duties" principle. Feature complexity is a selling point for a vendor in a competitive market but imposes unnecessary costs on a user organisation. Sometimes, this complexity of features comes about because a vendor's product suite is made up of disparate products brought together through various acquisitions, and the integration is consequently clunky and unnatural.

Custom Requirements: IAM is an area where every organisation has some unique requirements, and we provide two such examples in Appendices C and D. Not all specialised requirements can be met by simple configuration settings on a generic product, no matter what the brochures may tell you. Many of them will require some custom development. This has two logistical downsides in additional to a security implication that we cover separately in the next section.

One, your own in-house resources may be unable to make these changes because of their unfamiliarity with the new product, so you have to rely on vendor resources to make these changes for you. You will have to pay for the vendor's own consultants to work on your project and provide ongoing support for those customisations, and this is not something an organisation always budgets for at the outset.

Two, customised products are difficult to upgrade. When the vendor releases the next version of the product and your current version goes out of support, you will find it harder and costlier to migrate because of all the customisations you have made to the current version.

Closed Interfaces: The components of many brand-name products are often described as "tightly integrated". To a SOA-sensitised architect, the approving tone that usually accompanies this pejorative is a source of endless surprise and amusement. Tight integration in a product is not a desirable feature! It is a warning sign. Loose coupling is what we should be after.

What "tight integration" means in practice is that products only play well with others from the same stable. Many of them have proprietary "hooks" into complementary products even when open protocols would suffice. We know of one vendor whose interceptor component would only work in conjunction with their own policy/rules engine, which in turn was dependent on their specialised directory server. It was impossible to deploy one component without deploying at least two others, and interoperability with competing products was out of the question. This happens to a greater or lesser extent with all commercial vendors. It's part of their competitive DNA. Vendor lock-in also leads to a higher TCO (i.e., ongoing and switching costs, even if not up-front costs).

Conclusion: The combination of high upfront licence and consultancy fees, the tight coupling between components that complicates roll-outs and rules out incremental funding, the complexity of the product (impacting its understandability and maintainability), its impractical centralised model, the necessary customisations you need to make and the possibility of being locked into a particular vendor, contrasted with the simplicity of data design that can facilitate robust integration and the availability of a significant subset of IAM capability at commodity prices, should give you pause.

Well, this paper offers a much more attractive alternative. Our prescribed approach is simple:

1. Use the venerable architectural principle of "High Cohesion, Low Coupling" to identify the core functional components of an IAM system. Design loosely-coupled interfaces between them, often based on just data elements. Economy and agility follow from this principle.

2. Use Open Source components to deliver commoditised functionality (we'll name some good products you can use). There are many organisations that provide commercial support for these products for a reasonable annual fee, if you don't want to do it yourself.

3. You may find that the functionality gap to the simplest system that meets your requirements is quite bridgeable. Many of these requirements are necessarily specific to your organisation and we would be no better at predicting these than the big IAM vendors. So rather than hack an unfamiliar product to deliver that functionality, build it in the simplest way possible, using the tools your in-house developers know best. This is cheaper than using vendor consultants, maintenance is easier, and upgrades are on your own schedule with no artificial dependencies. We will identify some likely data structures and functions, and provide some tips on how to build these simply yet adequately.

We estimate that with this approach, you could save about 60%[9] of the cost of a comparable implementation using a brand-name commercial product.

---

[9] Our estimate is based on projections from empirical data that show that a 5-year roll-out of IAM at a medium-sized organisation (about 10 major applications, 5,000 employees and B2B users , and 100,000 customers) using a brand-name vendor product would cost about $5 million, while the approach we describe here would cost about $2 million. These are rough estimates, and your mileage will certainly vary, but we have no doubt the savings will be very significant.

Misconceptions about Security

While it's easy to mock organisations that blindly worship at the altar of big brand names, we also accept that there is some method in that madness. Big brand names are a convenient shorthand for compliance with the various security principles and standards that need to be followed in such an obviously risk-sensitive area.

Having said that, let us be under no illusions here. Even if you start with a certifiably secure product, as soon as you install it in your organisational environment, connect it to a couple of other systems, change a few configuration settings and customise some of its workflow, all that certification is moot. What may appear to a lay person (i.e., not a security specialist) as a trivial change could often introduce security holes into a previously secure system. Therefore, you will need to have *your particular implementation* audited and certified afresh. And this is not a one-time activity either but a periodic requirement, because changes are constantly applied to systems, and fresh security vulnerabilities could be introduced at any time in the application's lifecycle. There is no exemption from this procedure for organisations that implement an off-the-shelf product as opposed to an in-house build. At best, some subsystems that are untouched may be treated as black boxes. Keep in mind that a brand-name IAM product with a bunch of security standards certifications does not obviate the need for a security audit of your end-to-end system design[10].

The good news is that we're not necessarily starting off with no guidance or direction. There are many relevant security principles and standards that need to be followed in IAM, and we will demonstrate as we go along that the design we describe in this document is not a "cowboy" solution but an approach that is scrupulous in its adherence to security best practice.

For example, the Access Management side of IAM, which most requires the use of cryptographic techniques, is something we would not recommend writing in-house (unless your organisation specialises in writing security products). We recommend off-the-shelf, yet commoditised, products to perform these functions. The Single Sign-On ticketing server we recommend (CAS) provides various configuration points

---

[10] We're reasonably confident about the soundness of the approach we describe here because we had our system independently audited by an external consultancy. There were code and design reviews as well as penetration tests. Only after the review concluded with no serious findings did the system go live. You will almost certainly need to do the same with yours, regardless of whether you buy a vendor stack or "roll your own".

to enforce different aspects of security policy, such as token expiration, authentication throttling, and very high levels of cryptographic strength.

Some typical IAM-specific security requirements are listed in Appendix A, along with suggestions on how a LIMA-based system can support them.

In short, implementing IAM "on a shoestring" does not mean cutting corners on security. Far from it. Security is extremely important, as we will emphasise again and again. However, you should not allow anyone to use security as a bogeyman to scare you into paying much more for IAM than you really need to.

That's what this document is about.

Auditors, Security and Words of Wisdom

The proof of the security pudding is in the audit review, so to speak. However, security auditors will generally not sit down with you up front and help you design an IAM system, because it could compromise the independent stance they need to maintain. What they will probably do, though, is give you some principles to follow. Here are some that we learnt from our internal auditors:

Data Classification

- Levels of sensitivity

An organisation's data can be grouped into several categories, e.g., Public, Internal, Commercial-in-confidence, Confidential, Secret, etc. This categorisation is key to understanding the levels of access that should be granted to them, and should be carried out at the outset for any business system or application. Operations on data should also be categorised by sensitivity.

Access Management

- Secure-worthiness

In general, it is wasteful to expend effort to secure a resource beyond the value of the resource itself.

- Privacy

This relates to the confidentiality level of the data being considered. Encryption is one of the key mechanisms to ensuring privacy, and public key cryptography is a fairly standard technology used in IAM systems. Most of the security standards in the Identity Management area (AES, FIPS-140-2, etc.) pertain to cryptography.

- Least Privilege/Need to Know

Access should not be granted beyond the levels justified for a given purpose. The need to implement this uniformly then creates the justification for role-based access control mechanisms.

Identity Management

- Segregation of duties

One of the core principles in risk management is aimed at preventing corruption and fraud, by implementing proper controls. For example, a user cannot approve the request they have themselves made. This creates the justification for implementing two-step request/authorise functionality in IAM.

- Auditability

Any action that is deemed to be significant within a system needs to be logged with all relevant details surrounding it, – who did it and when, what was the purpose, who authorised it, etc. Audit logs need to be guaranteeably produced whenever such sensitive actions are performed, and the logs need to be secure against tampering or loss. Audit functions are a big part of an IAM system.

The Open Web Application Security Project (OWASP) lists a few more principles that you may want to cover off as well:
https://www.owasp.org/index.php/Category:Principle

Introducing LIMA[11] – A Different Architecture for IAM

Loose Coupling – A Firm Foundation for IAM

We've mentioned before that a major failing of big-name vendor products is the "tight integration" they feature. While "tight integration" means that components snap together readily, it could also mean they won't work without another component from the same vendor being present, or that they won't talk to third party components at all. These "lock-in" and "lock-out" consequences are the hidden costs of "tight integration".

The LIMA approach is consciously the opposite. We look for ways to decouple functions and retain the bare minimum functional dependency between them that is justifiable. Loose coupling makes it just as easy to "snap components together", but without the "lock-in" and "lock-out" disadvantages of proprietary interfaces. We have also learnt that appropriate data design can be a very effective way to achieve such loose coupling. We don't necessarily need a physical component to act as a decoupling intermediary.

User Identity

User Identity is the fundamental concept we are dealing with in an IAM system, and this can itself be treated in a decoupled manner with appropriate thought and design.

Tip 1: Identity references should be meaning-free

A major source of conceptual confusion comes from mistaking system accounts for user identity. A user may have a login account name of 'jbloggs' on a system, but this is just their identity *on that localised system*. It must not be conflated with a more global identity for that user. Even the user's login ID on the SSO server is not their identity, even though this is the identifier that grants them access to a

---

[11] The "IMA" part of LIMA stands for "Identity Management Architecture" of course, but you can choose to interpret the "L" as either "Low-cost", "Lightweight" or "Loosely-coupled", depending on whether your interest is economy, agility or architecture for its own sake.

multitude of systems. Any system-specific identifier is limiting because its scope is restricted.

Having a *meaning-free* identifier, on the other hand, provides tremendous flexibility. It can be *associated with* any set of identity attributes on any number of different systems. Those attributes and their mapping to this identifier can be modified quite easily to suit changing circumstances (e.g., a user changing their name or login ID on a system), and control can still be maintained.

So instead of linking attributes and meaning *directly* to a user's identity, make it meaning-free and associate it loosely with groups of attributes, including local identifiers on different systems.

Tip 2: A UUID is the most flexible meaning-free identifier

Universally Unique IDs (UUIDs) are extremely large numbers (128 bits long), traditionally expressed as 36-character hexadecimal strings[12]. UUIDs that are randomly generated have another very useful property. They are virtually guaranteed never to conflict, because their range of values is so large. Therefore, unlike sequence numbers, UUIDs don't have to be generated by a single source to guarantee their uniqueness. Multiple sources can simultaneously generate UUIDs, and they would still be guaranteeably unique. This becomes useful in IAM because more than one "upstream" system may provision new users.

Standardising on a UUID gives you the flexibility to let such upstream systems generate a UUID themselves and maintain a mapping from it to any local ID they may define. The treatment of user identity then becomes uniform from then on. You don't need to rely on a centralised component to provide unique identifiers to users from different provisioning sources.

Tip 3: Exploit the UUID to aid the audit function

One of the requirements of the audit function is to correlate activities performed on different systems. The challenge with traditional approaches is that when a message goes from one system to another, the user IDs on the two systems could be different, and the timestamps would also invariably be different. This makes it hard to prove that a log record on one system corresponds to a log record on another system. The User UUID is a good bridging mechanism. If each system logs

---

[12] A 128-bit integer would be expected to translate to a 32-character hexadecimal string, not 36. It's the convention though, to express UUIDs with hyphens separating groups of digits. E.g., 0fec5f44-1dc6-4b4e-8dd0-a5404520118d

the user's local ID and the UUID, it will be far easier to correlate activities across systems that belong to the same "thread" of execution. This doesn't remove the need for other correlating attributes like transaction IDs, but it strengthens the association of the activity with the user.

The other major advantage of including the UUID in log records is that the logs can be held on another system. Perhaps a centralised, enterprise logging service may in time replace the individual logging mechanisms of various systems, and you would then need to replace the system-specific identifiers with something global. Including the UUID reference from the start would make log records readily portable.

Identity versus Access

Identity refers to who someone is. Access refers to what they are allowed to do. While the two concepts are closely related, they are not the same. Therefore, they should not be coupled together more tightly than they need to be.

Tip 4: Decouple identity information from access control information

Following from Tip 1, treat the two groups of attributes relating to identity and access independently, and associate both of them with the user they refer to through a meaning-free identifier. In practical terms, this means the user repository that deals with authentication should be independent of the user repository that deals with authorisation. This counter-intuitive insight is explored in greater detail when we discuss the design of the IAM directory and database.

User Provisioning

The major benefit from automating user provisioning is the saved effort that would otherwise go towards setting users up on all the systems where they need to be defined. But almost by definition, this multi-system provisioning scheme needs to deal with multiple schemes for identifiers. Some older systems only take limited length numeric identifiers (e.g., "7634"), while others take longer alphanumeric ones (E.g., "jdoe" or "john.doe"). Still others may use email addresses as identifiers. Some are case-sensitive while others are not. It's not feasible to unify the schemes used for identifiers because of this diversity. A number of techniques could be used to manage this complexity, though.

Tip 5: User provisioning must exploit the mapping of UUIDs to local user IDs

Application systems need to set users up with IDs that conform to local schemes. However, it would be good if those local IDs could be mapped to a global, meaning-free ID and held within each system (as far as possible). There are a few complications here, as when downstream systems cannot hold references to UUIDs, and also when it is not possible for a provisioning message to know in advance what local user ID a user will be assigned on a system. These are explored in greater detail when we discuss user provisioning.

Opportunities for Loose Coupling in IAM

By breaking all the needless dependencies between functional components, as this diagram suggests, tremendous flexibility can be achieved, which translates into agility (time-to-value) and cost-effectiveness in development and operations.

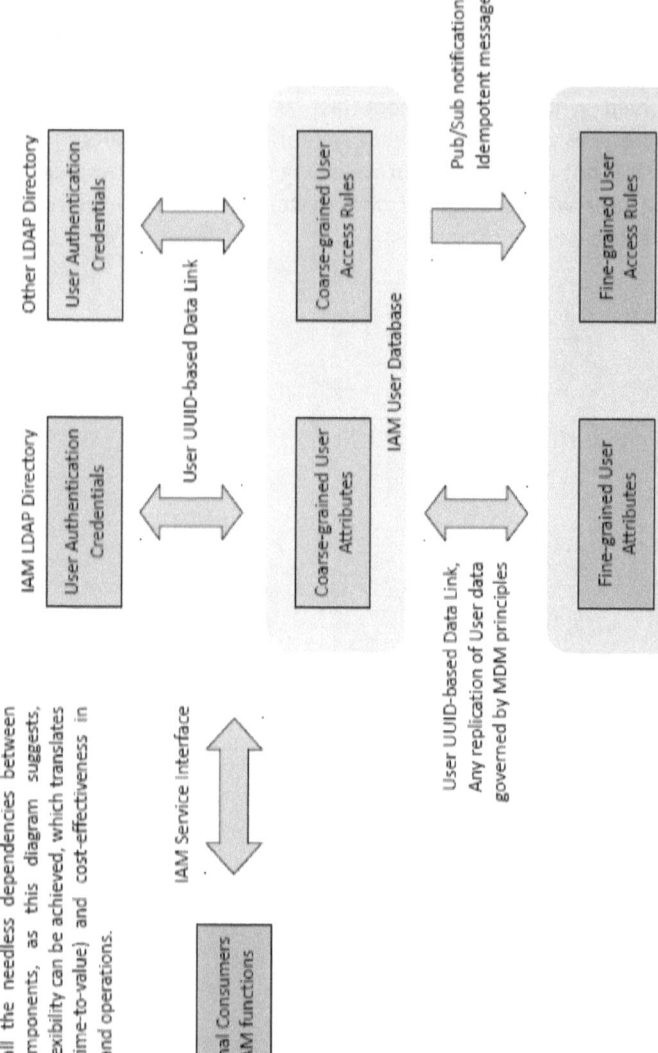

Fig 7: IAM – Opportunities for loose coupling

Sneak Preview – What a LIMA Implementation Looks Like

We will go into the details in later sections, but for now, this is a quick overview of some of the components a LIMA implementation may include.

Infrastructure:

- Use commodity infrastructure components – e.g., Intel x86_64 servers, Linux, Tomcat and stock-standard network devices that can filter accesses, perform network address translation and load-balance web servers. Higher-end infrastructure will generally cost you more without delivering any greater benefit. We discuss how to provide scalability and availability with an appropriate architecture.

- Use commodity directory, database and message queuing products. If you don't already have preferred products in these categories, OpenLDAP, MySQL (or PostgreSQL) and ActiveMQ are perfectly adequate Open Source offerings. There are some complications here for organisations that already use Microsoft's Active Directory, but we will cover that case a bit later.

Data design:

- It may be counter-intuitive, but you must use *both* an LDAP directory *and* a relational database, and split user data between them. Store only authentication credentials in the directory using the simplest possible tree structure and store all other attributes in the database[13]. The database design will be unique and specific to your organisation.

- Use a globally unique "User UUID" to associate multiple system accounts (application-specific user IDs) across different systems, including the IAM directory and database. This mapping provides the foundational capability to manage a user's attributes and access rights across multiple systems using a single, meaning-free identifier.

- Use a single "Person UUID" to associate multiple "User UUIDs". This provides the foundation to build sophisticated audit capabilities across multiple incarnations and engagements of the same physical user over a multi-year horizon.

---

[13] Our thanks to Stan Levine of Hyro Ltd for this extremely useful suggestion.

- Adopt a simple model for user roles and keep IAM's role-based access control tables relatively coarse-grained (e.g., application-level access rights only). Finer-grained roles within IAM to control access to application functions are neither necessary nor practical.

Access Management:

- Choose CAS (JA-SIG's Central Authentication Service product) as the heart of the Access Management solution. This is a ticket-based Single Sign-On system based on the Kerberos architecture but specially tuned for web applications. (We'll cover non-web applications later.)

- Shibboleth is a good choice for a federated identity solution, and we will describe its use in some detail.

- There is a wide choice of interceptors. CAS provides a servlet filter that you can simply configure and bundle with every web application. Or you can set up an authenticating reverse proxy that is common to a group of applications. There are other options as well.

Identity Management:

- Expose user administration functions as simple REST-based services. Upstream "sources of truth" for user data such as HR applications and resource management systems should initiate user provisioning/de-provisioning and the grant and revocation of user access rights by invoking these services. You can secure access to these HTTP-based services using IAM's own Access Management capability.

- Build simple user administration screens using an agile toolkit of your choice (e.g., Grails, Roo) that can also reuse these REST services.

- The invocation of REST services and the use of user administration screens may require "user events" to be generated downstream in addition to local updates to the IAM directory and database.

- The interaction between upstream systems and IAM need be no more complex than synchronous request/response. However, the interaction between IAM and downstream systems needs to be asynchronous and loosely-coupled for maximum flexibility. These aspects are described below.

- Implement user provisioning to applications downstream of IAM using an event notification mechanism rather than tightly-coupled service calls. To make them future-proof, keep the "user event" messages generic rather than tailored to each downstream application. Using persistent messages, durable subscriptions and listeners on all target applications, changes to user data can be managed across the enterprise in a flexible, reliable and robust manner. Applications can be added or decommissioned at any point in the system's lifetime without any downtime.

- Make your provisioning messages idempotent, for a really simple reliability mechanism. The ability to retry an operation without danger of duplication is very powerful and liberating.

- Where responses are required from downstream systems, use the same notification mechanism with separate "user event acknowledgement" messages that only IAM listens for.

- Errors encountered by downstream systems when processing user events must be handled in a decoupled way. A separate error reporting mechanism, even a separate error queue, is preferable. User event notification, acknowledgement responses and errors are not to be treated as they would be in synchronous request/response systems. This is an important aspect of loose coupling that keeps the Identity Management solution simple and modular.

These are the basic ingredients of a cost-effective IAM solution, and we will describe and explain them in detail in the rest of this document.

The following diagrams illustrate the logical and physical components of LIMA.

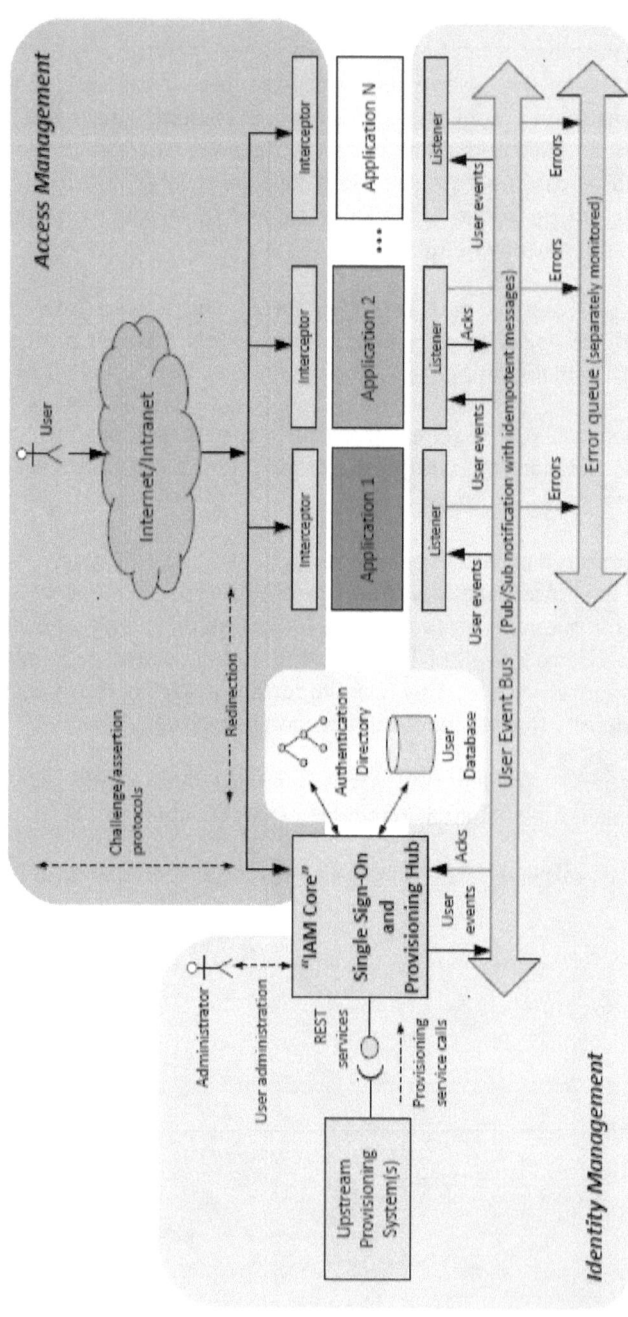

Fig 8: Logical components of LIMA

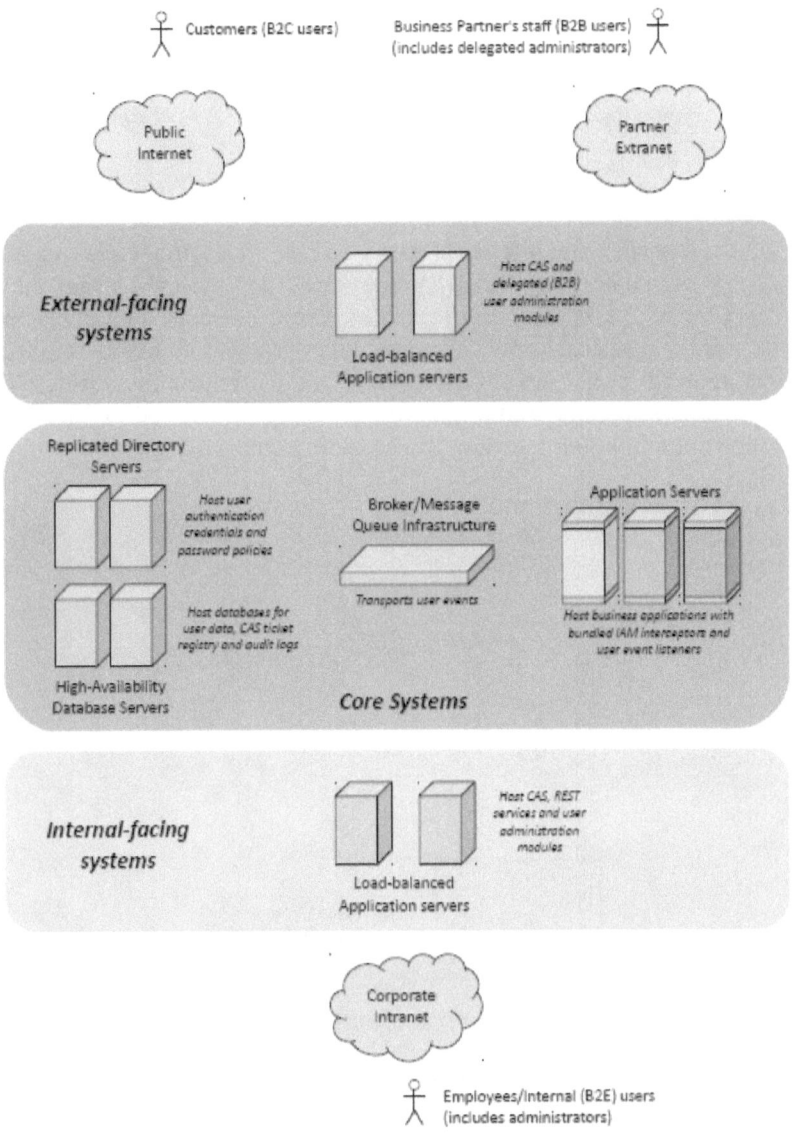

Fig 9: Physical components of LIMA

Access Management, LIMA-style

Let's now go through the detailed conceptual steps that build up to the solution above.

Access Management Concepts

Take Access Management first. Let's say we want to control access to a web application. The simplest model is when the application itself challenges the user for credentials (e.g., asks for a user ID and password by popping up a login page) and validates them against its own database before allowing access to its functions. The application performs both authentication ("Is the user who they claim to be?") using the password, and authorisation ("Is the user allowed to access this information or perform this function?") using stored access rules.

The diagram below illustrates this.

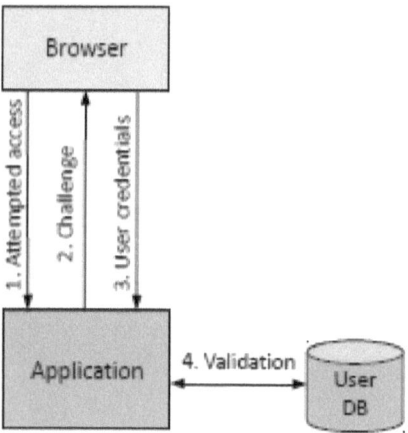

Fig 10: Standalone authentication

While this is a simple model, it becomes operationally cumbersome when an organisation has many such applications. Each application needs to maintain an independent set of credentials, which means users may need to remember many user IDs and passwords. It becomes logistically expensive to manage user data consistently across multiple systems, to "provision" new users or to "de-provision" them when they leave the organisation. Processes are necessarily manual and

Identity Management on a Shoestring

error-prone. Security policies are not uniformly applied across all applications. The list goes on.

A simple extension is to have all applications validate user credentials against a common repository, most frequently an enterprise LDAP directory. Here's what the picture then looks like:

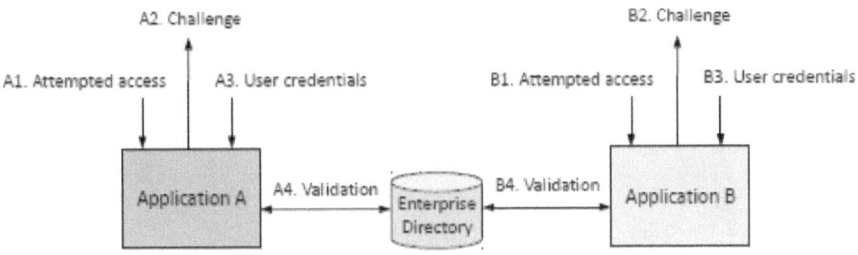

Fig 11: Delegated authentication

This is somewhat better because applications can now delegate the management of user credentials (and even access rights) to an external component. User credentials are held in and validated against a single repository (i.e., centralised authentication). When access rights are also similarly held and validated, this is centralised authorisation. User provisioning and de-provisioning are a lot simpler because only one data store needs to be managed. Security policies are more consistent across applications because they are essentially defined at a single point (although enforcement is still at each application's discretion).

From an auditor's perspective, although this is progress, it is still not guaranteeably secure because enforcement of enterprise security policies, however well defined, is still left to individual applications. Moreover, it still isn't as convenient to users as it could be, because it isn't really "Single Sign-On". True, users now only have to remember one set of credentials, but they have to enter them afresh when accessing each application they use. It's more "Single set of credentials" than "Single Sign-On". Can something be done about these points? In other words, can the enforcement and challenge parts of the process be delegated to an external component as well?

The answer is yes, and modern Access Management systems do exactly this.

Delegating the challenge for user credentials is done as follows. The application needs to *redirect* the browser, on initial access, to a centralised component (the SSO server), which performs the challenge and validation steps before redirecting the browser back (transparently) to the application. If the user credentials are not valid, the SSO server will essentially block this access. The application now trusts the identity of the user that is passed in, because this has been vetted by a trusted system.

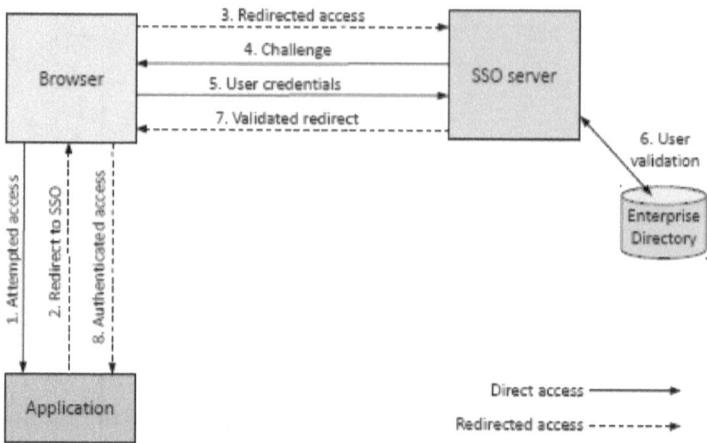

Fig 12: Basic Single Sign-On (SSO)

This delegation provides true "Single Sign-On", and we will shortly explain why a second login is not required for subsequent accesses to other applications. However, enforcement of access control is still left to the application, and the delegation of this function is typically addressed using a dedicated security "interceptor".

The interceptor is a component that sits in front of an application and redirects access to the SSO server. It may also perform the access control (authorisation) function based on the user identity and any other user attributes sent back by the SSO server. The application is then completely agnostic to the presence of the authentication and authorisation functions that are being performed[14]. A specialised interceptor component not only relieves the application from having to implement these aspects of security, it can be treated as part of the enterprise security framework and is also a more easily auditable control point. This is illustrated in the following diagram.

---

[14] In practice, the application will still perform *fine-grained* authorisation ("i.e., Can the user perform this function?") based on the user attributes passed in, but authentication and *coarse-grained* authorisation (i.e., "Can the user access this application at all?") are done by the SSO server and interceptor, respectively.

Identity Management on a Shoestring

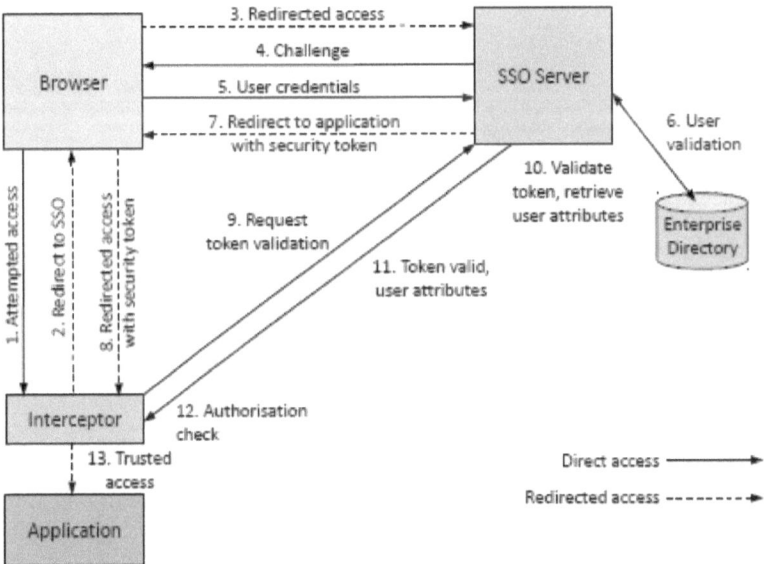

Fig 13: Comprehensive SSO

Note that we need the extra steps 9, 10 and 11 to make this fool-proof. The interceptor has to perform a further level of validation against the SSO engine to ensure that the security token is genuine. The SSO server needs to confirm the authenticity of the token. It may also send back extra user attributes along with this confirmation. The interceptor uses these attributes to enforce access control rules (authorisation). And with this, the access management model is complete.

There are some details that need to be understood about this essentially simple model. There are two types of security tokens required to make this system work. The first is related to authentication and the second is an "application access token" that is loosely related to authorisation. In fact, because authentication is for the user but access relates to the user and an application, only one authentication token is generated per user but there will be as many access tokens as there are applications that the user wants to access.

A diagram will explain this.

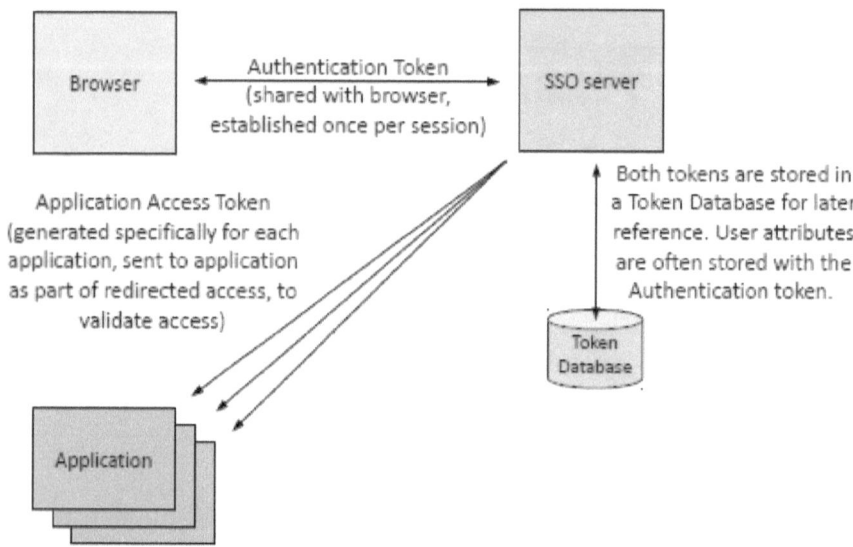

Fig 14: Authentication and access tokens

The authentication token is generated by the SSO server once the user is authenticated. As the diagram above shows, the SSO server shares this token with the user's browser[15]. If the browser presents this token to the SSO server again (within a reasonable time window), the SSO server will not demand a fresh login and authentication cycle. This is Single Sign-On, of course. We'll see the details of how this works in the next section, but note that both types of tokens are stored by the SSO server in a token database, because they will need to be retrieved for validation later.

The application-specific access token for a user and application is generated after authentication. This second token (or more specifically, the handle or ID of the token) needs to accompany the redirected request back to the application, and the application's interceptor will need to have it validated by the SSO server to prevent spoofing. That's why it needs to be saved in the token database.

---

[15] This is usually a session cookie, and we'll see more of this when discussing the CAS product.

As we have seen, the interceptor may also use the user identity and other attributes to perform an authorisation check before allowing the user in[16].

As we will see in our discussion of CAS, a common optimisation is for user attributes retrieved when authenticating access to the first application, to be stored with the Authentication Token in the token database. This allows the SSO server to send user attributes to each application's interceptor without having to retrieve them repeatedly from the user repository.

---

[16] It is also possible to ensure that the application access token is only generated by the SSO server after it performs this authorisation itself. So verifying and enforcing authorisation rules may be done either by the SSO server or by the interceptor, and both are optional in any case, which is why we said this token is only loosely related to authorisation.

How Single Sign-On Works

To understand how SSO works, let's see what happens when a user accesses a second application within the Single Sign-On environment after having been successfully authenticated and granted access to the first one. Follow carefully the flows in the diagram below. It may look complex at first glance, but follows quite simply from what we have seen earlier.

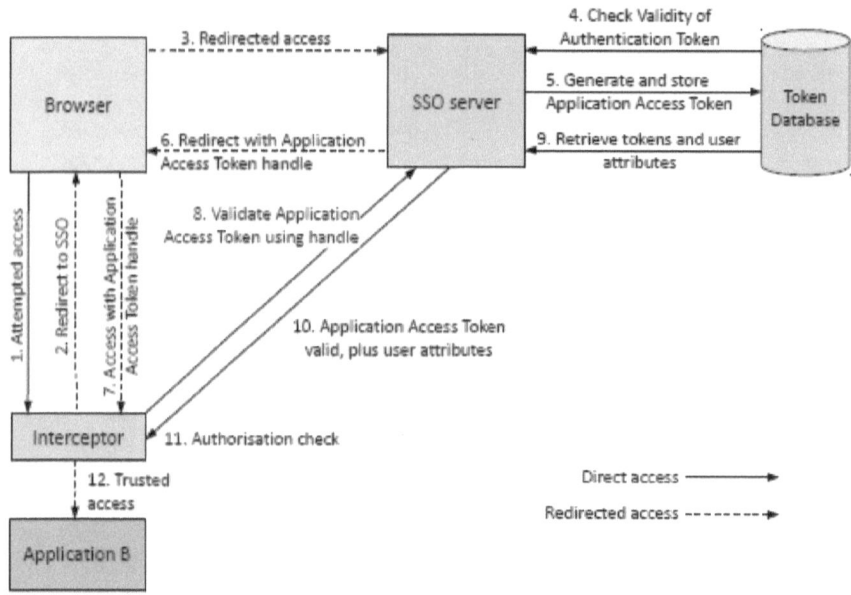

Fig 15: SSO steps

What is happening here?

When the interceptor redirects the browser to the SSO server, the browser produces the Authentication Token that the SSO server gave it at the time of its first login (when the browser tried to access the first application). The SSO server checks the validity of the Authentication Token against its Token Database. If the token is valid, it means the Single Sign-On session is still active and the user doesn't have to log in again. So the user will not see a login screen this time. This is SSO!

What about authorisation? Well, there are a few options on how this can be done. The diagram above shows how coarse-grained authorisation works in the general case. The SSO server generates an Application Access Token for this application anyway, stores it in the Token Database and then redirects the browser back to the application along with the token's "handle", usually as a URL parameter. As before, when the application's interceptor receives the token handle, it checks back with the SSO server to see if this is genuine and still valid. The SSO server retrieves the full token from its Token Database based on the "handle" and validates it. The Application Access Token is also linked to the Authentication Token, which has a bunch of user attributes stored along with it. The SSO server passes all of this back to the interceptor. If the Application Access token is certified to be valid, the interceptor may apply authorisation checks based on the user attributes accompanying the response, and then allow or disallow access to the application as a whole. This is coarse-grained authorisation. The interceptor may also pass these user attributes through to the business application for it to do any fine-grained authorisation.

In a later section, we will see how to implement simple extensions to the challenge protocol to exploit the existing Windows-based LAN session, support multi-factor authentication and also federated identity systems. We will also explore a more tailored version of coarse-grained authorisation. However, the model described here is all there is to Access Management, so it is conceptually quite simple.

We stated earlier that Access Management is also the most commoditised part of IAM, so let's now look at two of the best (and cheapest) products you can find to implement Access Management.

Ganesh Prasad and Umesh Rajbhandari

The Best Things in Life (and in IAM) are Free

If you're looking for a secure and tested product to implement the Ticketing Server-based Single Sign-On Access Management model that we just described, then CAS (JA-SIG's Central Authentication Service) is far and away the simplest and least expensive.

Likewise, if you're looking for a *federated*[17] Single Sign-On Access Management solution, you cannot do better than Shibboleth[18].

Both of these are Open Source, which means there are no licence fees, but more importantly, that there are no hidden hooks or dependencies (our infamous "tight integration") to lock you into the product and lock out competing vendors' products. You will find that integration and operational costs, more than licence costs, are the real arguments in favour of an Open Source solution.

If you have strong Java support skills in your own organisation, then the only ongoing cost of implementing these products is the cost of the staff dedicated to supporting them. However, most organisations would also prefer to back up such front-line support with some kind of commercial support agreement (second- and third-level support). Here again, because of the Open Source nature of these products, you are very likely to find companies that understand and are willing to support them for a reasonable annual fee[19].

---

[17] We have a rather simple and practical definition of federated identity management as opposed to local identity management. If you provision user data (including authentication credentials) into repositories, for your own organisation's use, then all you need is local identity management. But if you have to grant access to users who you do not yourself provision but rely on other organisations to vouch for, or if other organisations need you to vouch for users in *your* repositories who will access *their* systems, then what you need is a federated identity system. In both these cases, one organisation trusts another to vouch for users who are not provisioned in the first organisation's repository.

[18] Why not just use Shibboleth for everything, since its capabilities are obviously a superset of CAS's? Shibboleth is a more complex product than CAS to install, maintain and roll out, so if you don't need federated identity, you're probably best off using just CAS. Even if federated identity is part of your requirement, we discuss a couple of ways in which you can keep the consequent complexity restricted to only a part of your infrastructure.

[19] An organisation used to traditional commercial software support agreements would very likely be pleasantly surprised at the support rates they are likely to be quoted for Open Source products.

With both CAS and Shibboleth, the SSO ticketing model works roughly analogously:

1. A client application (browser) attempts to access a business application

2. There is an interceptor of some sort that redirects the browser to an SSO server. With Shibboleth, locating the SSO server is a little more involved because it's not a local system.

3. The SSO server challenges the browser to provide user authentication credentials.

4. Once the browser has submitted these credentials and the SSO server has validated them in some way, it generates an Authentication Token and an Application Access Token of its own and redirects the browser back to the business application with the handle of the Application Access Token. (The Authentication Token is given to the browser to store as a session cookie and produce each time it returns to the SSO server.)

5. The interceptor again blocks the redirected request and finds the handle of the Application Access Token. It issues a confirmation query to the SSO server internally (without redirecting the request through the browser) to check if this is a valid token.

6. If the SSO server confirms the validity of the token, the interceptor allows access to the application, after optionally checking the accompanying user attributes.

Central Authentication Service and the CAS Protocol

In the 1980s, MIT developed an authentication system for distributed applications that would work even over an untrusted network. The protocol was called Kerberos, and it has since become the most successful Single Sign-On mechanism used in the industry.

Yale University then took the Kerberos idea and implemented a version called CAS, tailored to web applications. While the tokens used in CAS are not *kerberized* tickets (i.e., they don't use the same formats that Kerberos does), the types of components and the sequence of interactions between them is an exact analogue of Kerberos.

CAS is a product that is extremely popular in academia, with most major universities using it to secure their websites and web applications and provide Single Sign-On to them. However, it has not been as popular in corporate circles, and the reason for that is probably just corporate snobbery with regard to academia! There is certainly nothing deficient in the product that either we or our auditors could find. We believe you will find CAS to be an extremely efficient, secure and maintainable piece of software.

Here is the Kerberos/CAS authentication model at a glance, using the appropriate terminology:

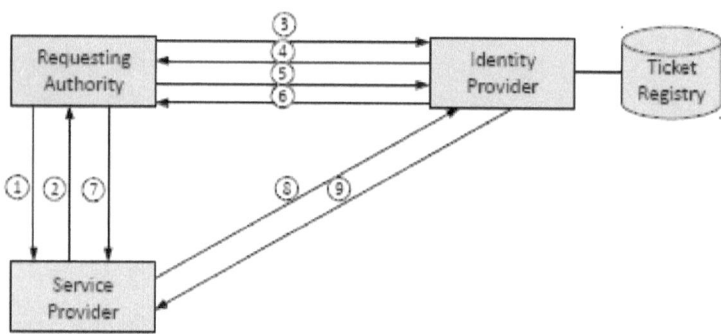

Fig 16: Kerberos/CAS model

1. The Requesting Authority (RA), which could be any application but specifically a browser in the CAS implementation, tries to access an application (the Service Provider or SP). The SP is nothing but a web application in the CAS model.

2. The Service Provider has no way of authenticating the RA or of trusting any credentials that the RA may present to it directly. So it redirects the RA to an Identity Provider (IdP) that it trusts, and will only accept a proof of authentication from that trusted source. With CAS, this is a simple HTTP redirect to the URL of the IdP, with the URL of the SP appended. The latter URL is required because the IdP needs to be able to redirect the RA back to the original SP after successful validation of the RA's credentials.

3. The RA follows the redirect and accesses the IdP. With CAS, since the URL contains the SP's URL, the IdP knows which application is being accessed.

4. The IdP challenges the RA to provide authentication credentials. In the case of CAS, this is usually just a login page that employs HTTP Form-based Authentication.

5. The RA submits its credentials to the IdP. With CAS, a user fills in the login page with a user ID and password and submits the form. The form submission is over HTTPS for security.

At this point, the IdP validates the user's credentials against a repository (usually an LDAP directory). If the credentials are valid[20], the IdP generates two tokens – the Authentication Token is called a "Ticket-Granting Ticket" (TGT), which is the Single Sign-On token. Production of this token by the RA within a certain session duration means the RA will not have to log in afresh. The Application Access Token is called a "Service Ticket" (ST) that the Service Provider requires if it has to allow the RA access to its functions. In CAS, the TGT is a session cookie while the handle to the ST is a string appended to the application's URL. The tickets are also stored in a local Ticket Registry for future reference, as will be seen[21]. The TGT is typically stored for a few hours because that defines the length of an SSO session, while the ST only needs to be stored for a few seconds or a couple of minutes until the SP asks to verify its validity.

---

[20] If the credentials are not valid, CAS can be configured to simply display the login page again. This can continue until the directory server locks out the user account.
[21] CAS can be extended to retrieve any additional user attributes from a user repository after authentication, and to store these attributes along with the TGT in a "blob" attribute that is meant for this purpose. This is done just once at initial login, and these user attributes can thenceforth be retrieved from the Ticket Registry on each subsequent application access, saving a fresh user repository access each time.

6. The IdP sends both tokens to the RA. With CAS, this is another HTTP redirect. The Ticket-Granting Ticket is placed in a session cookie that is only shared between the RA and the IdP and never with any SP. The redirect URL is the SP's URL which was appended to the original redirect to the IdP in step 2. In addition, CAS appends the ST's handle to the URL as a standard URL parameter.

7. The RA follows the redirect instruction and accesses the SP again. This time, the ST handle is part of the URL. The TGT is not sent to the SP because that is a cookie shared only between the browser and the IdP.

   The SP picks up the Service Ticket handle from the URL but has no way to verify its authenticity.

8. The SP sends the ST handle to the IdP to validate it. In CAS, this is a direct HTTP call (not redirected through the browser since the RA is not yet trusted at this point).

   The IdP uses the ST handle to retrieve the ST from its Ticket Registry and validate it. The ST does not need to be held in the Ticket Registry for more than a few seconds, because the verification request from the SP typically comes in almost immediately after the IdP sends the RA the redirect request containing the ST handle. The ST has a reference to the TGT, so the IdP also retrieves the TGT with its associated user attributes.

9. The IdP sends back a response to the SP verifying the authenticity of the ST[22] along with the user attributes it has retrieved. At this point, the RA is authenticated. The SP uses these ser attributes to decide whether to grant access to its functions or not.

The CAS website provides plenty of detailed technical material: http://www.jasig.org/cas

---

[22] The Service Ticket validation message sent back by CAS is accompanied by the user attributes that were stored in the Ticket Registry as a "blob" attribute of the TGT. This approach saves a separate database access during the performance-critical login process. We used an XML structure in the response body to transport attributes but any suitable data format can be used.

Identity Management on a Shoestring

Shibboleth's Federated Identity Model

In many ways, Shibboleth's industry street-cred is better than CAS's, which, as we have mentioned, is unfairly viewed as a product for academic institutions. Three disparate federated identity schemes (Liberty ID-FF, Shibboleth and the earlier SAML 1.1) fed into the recent SAML2 specification. Many of the spec writers were Shibboleth developers, and this must have played no small part in ensuring the close match between the SAML2 standard and the Shibboleth implementation. Open Source has thus managed to gain the inside track on federated identity. Any commercial product that claims compatibility with the SAML2 spec is by definition interoperable with Shibboleth. The implication is that interoperability with business partners is not a concern that should stand in the way of your implementing Shibboleth for your federated identity management capability.

Here is how Shibboleth works. Keep in mind our earlier description of a ticketing server-based SSO solution as well as the CAS model, and you will see the main differences.

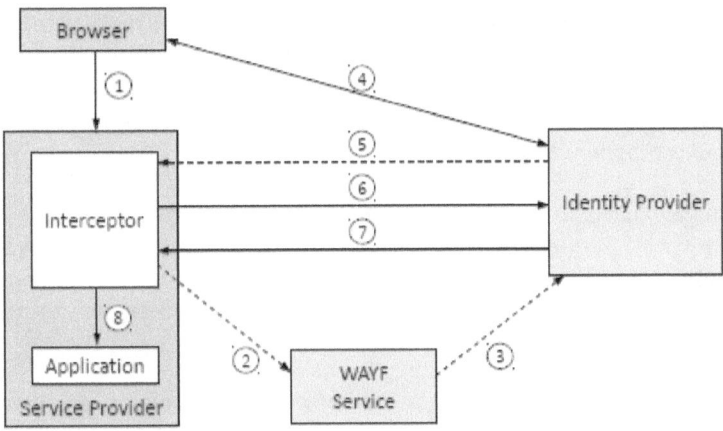

Fig 17: Shibboleth model

1. The browser attempts to access the business application protected by an interceptor. This combination is referred to as the Service Provider (SP).

2. The interceptor may redirect the browser to a service called WAYF (Where Are You From), which determines the appropriate Identity Provider (IdP) for the user. However, the IdP can also be resolved using a number of different mechanisms.

3. The browser is then redirected to that Identity Provider. This usually belongs to the user's "home organisation", where they have been provisioned and where their authentication credentials are stored.

4. The Identity Provider challenges the user to provide the appropriate authentication credentials for that organisation and receives those credentials. This could again use any number of challenge/assertion protocols.

5. After successful authentication, a set of tokens is generated for this session, and the browser is redirected back to the Service Provider with a service token.

6. The interceptor requests the Identity Provider to validate the service token and queries for user attributes.

7. The Identity Provider validates the service token and provides user attribute information as per its attribute release policy.

8. If the token is valid and the user's attributes also conform to the application's specified requirements, the interceptor grants access to the application.

As you can see, the federated access management model is virtually identical to the local one in its general outline, with the only additional feature being the WAYF service that resolves the correct Identity Provider to use. Within a local context, every interceptor knows the location of the SSO server, so there is no need for a specialised component to perform this resolution function.

The main complexity in Shibboleth is the requirement to set up a Service Provider capability at each business application node, which is a lot more onerous than the equivalent simple CAS interceptor. Therefore, you wouldn't want to use Shibboleth in preference to CAS unless you have a legitimate requirement for federated identity[23].

Let's look at CAS in greater detail now. Although CAS is simple, it can be enhanced with very little effort to cover a number of different Access Management situations, such as integration with Windows-based LANs and Two-Factor Authentication for applications requiring greater security. We will show how this can be done using case studies.

---

[23] With the increasing popularity of cloud-based solutions, this could become a common requirement very soon. Not every cloud-based system requires federated identity, though. We cover this subtle point in a later discussion on Cloud Computing.

It's only when we start to talk about federated identity that Shibboleth needs to come into the picture. We will look at federated identity and its unique requirements later using a specific case study.

A good external reference to Shibboleth:
http://www.jisc.ac.uk/whatwedo/themes/accessmanagement/federation/shibbolethdemo.aspx

CAS Server Configuration and the "Two-Layer Protocol Architecture"

Here are some tips for setting up CAS as your SSO server.

Tip 1: Cater for high availability of the IAM solution

IAM can become the single point of failure for all your applications unless you take steps to ensure its availability. You would of course set up your directory in a replicated configuration, and your database is also likely to be set up in HA (High Availability) mode. But what about the SSO server?

CAS servers are stateless (i.e., they maintain no data in session state), so there is no need to cluster them. A load-balanced configuration is sufficient to provide high availability. Any standard hardware-based load-balancer will do nicely, as shown below:

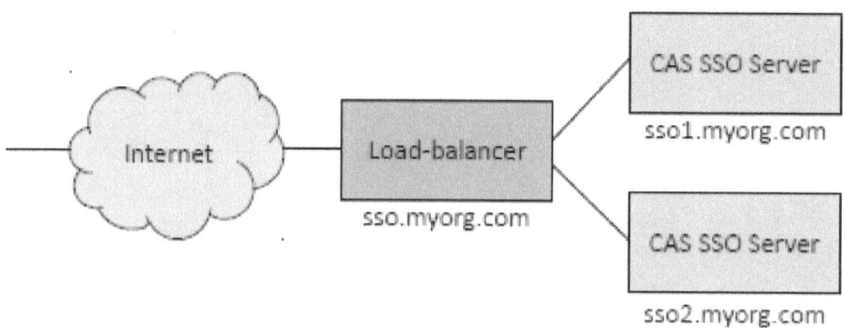

Fig 18: SSO load-balancing

Tip 2: Don't reveal your SSO implementation through your domain naming scheme

As the diagram above suggests, keep your domain names technology-neutral. When an application's interceptor redirects a browser to CAS, the browser will display the URL of the CAS server (or more correctly, the URL of the load-balancer) at the top of the SSO login page. As long as this says something neutral like "sso.myorg.com" and not "cas.myorg.com", it will not provide any clues about the actual product being used to implement SSO. It is prudent to avoid revealing details of your organisation's implementation in case a hacker exploits a known vulnerability in the product at some future date.

Tip 3: Share repositories between internal- and external-facing CAS servers

While CAS is stateless (i.e., no in-memory state), it does reference data in three data stores, i.e., the directory, the user database and the ticket registry.

Sharing the directory and database makes sense because you can provision all users to a single repository and have them access either internal- or external-facing applications, from either within the corporate LAN or from outside. A suitable directory structure as we will describe later can support all types of access.

Similarly, sharing the ticket registry can also make sense. In certain use cases, it may be necessary to grant access to an application that is normally internal-facing to an external user or vice-versa. Having a shared ticket registry can ensure that SSO spans both internal and external systems with no additional effort.

Tip 4: Most importantly, try and adopt a "Two-Layer Protocol Architecture" and use CAS to hide the various challenge/assertion protocols required, from application interceptors

As we will see in the next three sections, we often have a requirement for other "challenge/assertion" protocols to authenticate users. Rather than complicate the entire Access Management infrastructure to support these varied protocols, we suggest a simple "Two-Layer Protocol Architecture" that looks like this:

Layer 1: The CAS protocol should be the sole "internal" protocol seen by application interceptors, i.e., they will expect CAS service tickets with every initial access from a browser and will redirect the browser to a CAS server if they don't find one. They will also make a validation request to the CAS server to verify the authenticity of every service ticket presented to them.

Layer 2: The CAS server (and any associated products) will manage the various "external" challenge/assertion protocols that may be required.

The Two-Layer Protocol Architecture is illustrated below:

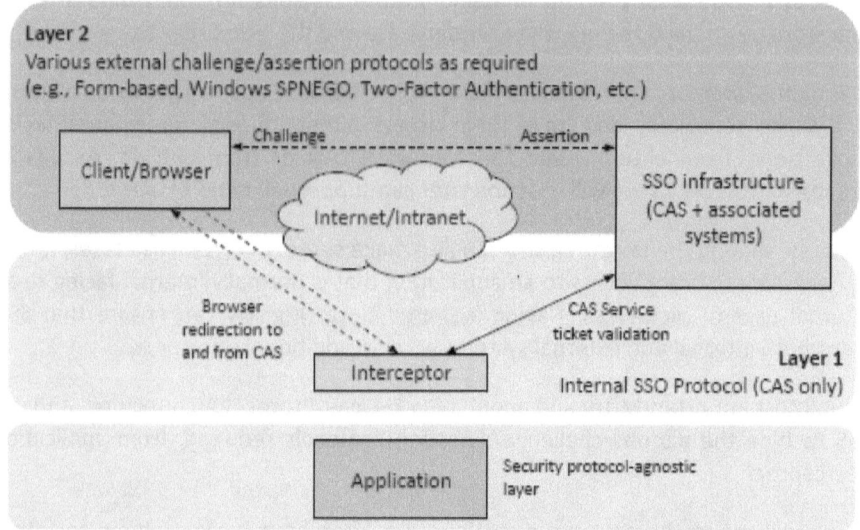

Fig 19: Two-Layer Protocol Architecture

The next three sections will illustrate the utility of the Two-Layer Protocol Architecture when we extend our Access Management infrastructure to cover three different situations:

1. LAN-based Single Sign-On using SPNEGO
2. Two-Factor Authentication using SMS One-Time Tokens
3. Federated Identity using SAML2[24]

---

[24] There is a potential problem with using the Two-Layer Protocol Architecture for federated identity situations, which we will cover when we get to that discussion.

Enhancing Access Management Functionality Incrementally

Let's see how the LIMA approach, especially the Two-Layer Protocol Architecture for Access Management, can help you painlessly enhance the functionality of your IAM system to cater to additional requirements.

Extension Case Study 1: LAN SSO Integration with SPNEGO

A frequent requirement, especially for intranet applications, is to exploit the fact that the user has already logged into the corporate LAN through their Windows workstation login screen. There should be no need to log in again to a web-based application. Without LAN integration, even web-based Single Sign-On implies two logins, which is not ideal.

The solution lies in a Microsoft protocol called SPNEGO (Simple and Protected Negotiation), by which a web application can transparently query the browser for a token from the Windows security environment which it can verify against Active Directory. So without the user having to log in again explicitly, the system can perform an authentication and thereby secure web applications by leveraging the earlier LAN authentication[25].

---

[25] SPNEGO refers to the negotiation protocol. The actual authentication protocol, which is invisible at the level we are interested in, is either NTLM or Kerberos.

The following figure illustrates the way SPNEGO would work in the straightforward case:

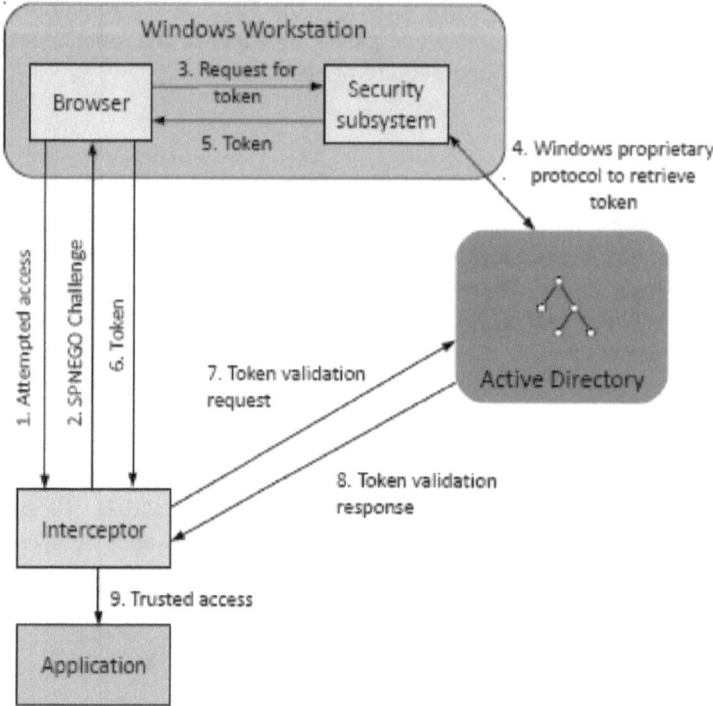

Fig 20: Straightforward SPNEGO

In our experience, the same web application may have to support both internal (LAN) users as well as external users (B2B and B2C) who do not have a prior Windows LAN login session. Implementing the model above would mean that an application (or its interceptor) would need to understand and implement two different protocols (SPNEGO and CAS) to cater to these two sets of users.

As we suggested in the last section, a Two-Layer Protocol Architecture can alleviate this complexity. The application interceptors only understand CAS as always. The CAS server itself is capable of issuing an SPNEGO challenge and validating the token presented by the browser, so SPNEGO should be *delegated* to the CAS server, as shown below:

Step 1:

The browser attempts to access the application and the CAS interceptor redirects it to the CAS SSO server as usual.

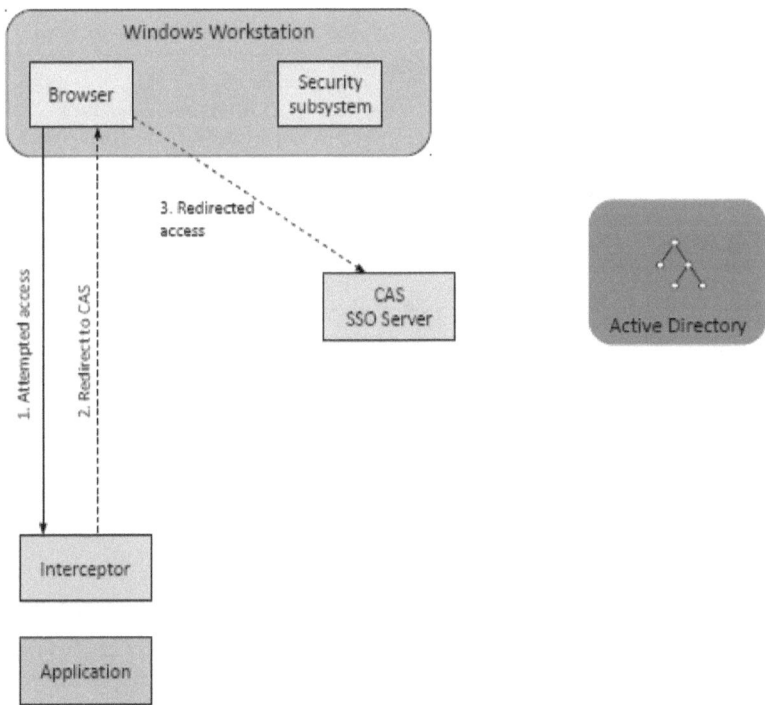

Fig 21: CAS SPNEGO Step 1

The default behaviour of CAS is to try various types of authentication mechanisms in a particular order (as specified in a configuration file) until one of them successfully authenticates the user. For example, CAS can try SPNEGO first and if that fails, it can display a login form. Alternatively, the interceptor can provide a hint of some sort to CAS that this access requires to be authenticated through SPNEGO rather than a login form. We'll talk about a simple way to do this at the end of this discussion.

Step 2:

Now *CAS* issues the SPNEGO challenge, receives the token from the browser and validates it against Active Directory.

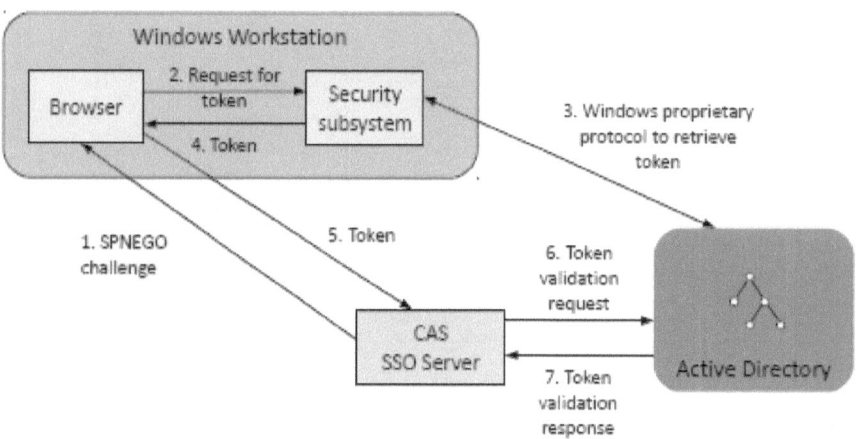

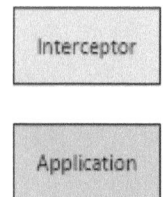

Fig 22: CAS SPNEGO Step 2

At this stage, the situation is very similar to the standard CAS protocol at the point where CAS has just succeeded in authenticating the user against the directory. From here on, the sequence of events resembles the standard CAS protocol.

Step 3:

The CAS server generates its two tokens (Ticket-Granting Ticket and Service Ticket) before redirecting the browser back to the application. The interceptor receives the Service Ticket as part of the redirected access request and validates it against CAS. CAS retrieves user attributes stored in the Ticket Registry and sends a response back to the interceptor. If everything checks out, access is granted.

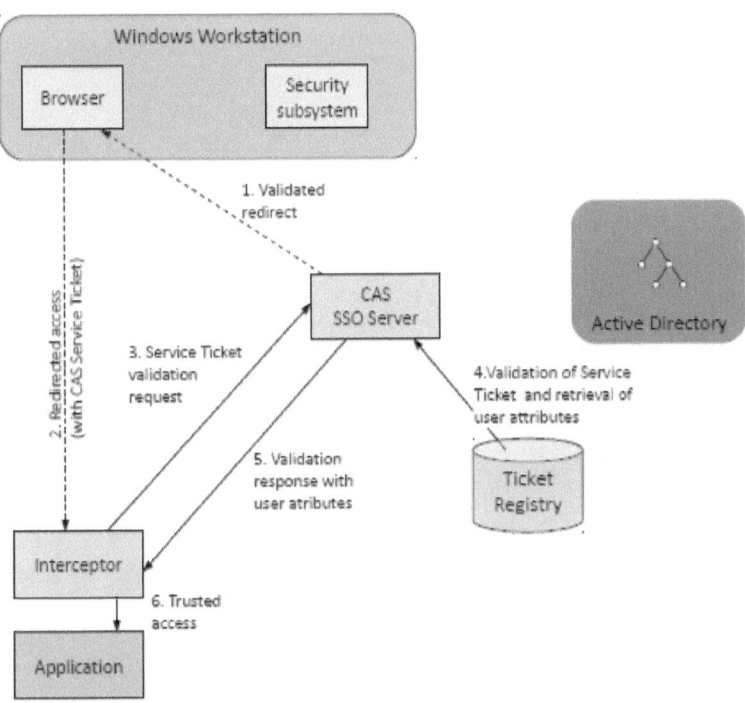

Fig 23: CAS SPNEGO Step 3

From the perspective of the interceptor, the only protocol it has to know about is CAS. The domain names can be set up so that internal (LAN) users and external users access the application through two slightly different URLs. This difference in URLs is all the hint that CAS requires to use different challenge protocols for the two types of user.

We recommend the same architectural approach when supporting any other challenge/assertion protocol. Keep the interceptor logic simple and standard (i.e., based on CAS). Delegate the actual challenge/validation logic to the centralised server. This way, all complexity is contained within a single unit (the SSO server) rather than dispersed across the network. Applications and their interceptors are all standard regardless of the kind of authentication protocol used.

Extension Case Study 2: Two-Factor Authentication with SMS One-Time Tokens

Sometimes, web applications have the requirement for "Two-Factor Authentication" for extra security. In other words, the user is expected to produce two independent sets of credentials to be successfully authenticated. Two-Factor Authentication is also described as "what you have and what you know". This is more secure than merely having two passwords, because two passwords can be stolen as easily as one, but two factors are harder for a malicious user to steal from a legitimate user than one, because a physical object has to be stolen in addition to a piece of information.

There are many forms of Two-Factor Authentication[26], but what we will illustrate here is a simple scheme involving a mobile phone (what the user has) and a password (what the user knows).

Remember that CAS is an Open Source product with several customisation/extension points, making it easy to add the functionality we need. One of these extension points is the login screen. We will touch on the ability to customise the login screen using stylesheets specific to a partner organisation later on, but the customisation that we will use here is a change of screen flow[27].

CAS uses Spring Web Flow internally, so any Java web developer with knowledge of Spring Web Flow should find it easy to make the change we describe below.

The idea behind this implementation of Two-Factor Authentication is that every user of the protected business application has a mobile phone that they always carry with them. They also know their Single Sign-On password. The CAS server will prompt them for a user ID and password as always, but instead of generating tickets and letting them into the application upon successful authentication, it will also test for their possession of their mobile phone at that point in time, and grant access only if they can prove it.

---

[26] CAS already supports authentication through either passwords or X.509 certificates. With a simple code tweak, it can be made to require both, thereby providing another implementation of Two-factor Authentication.

[27] Keep in mind that although the change we describe should not negatively impact security, it will need to be documented and the new design reviewed by auditors before it can go into production. The auditors must confirm that the extension implemented does not compromise the basic CAS security protocol in any way, since it is only meant to add an extra authentication step before tickets are generated.

For this to work, the user will have to have been provisioned earlier on in the IAM database with their mobile phone number as an important attribute. As soon as CAS successfully authenticates the user against the LDAP directory, it retrieves the user's mobile phone number from the database. It also generates a One-Time Token (OTT), e.g., a random number of (say) 6 digits, stores the OTT temporarily in the database against the user record along with a timestamp, and sends the OTT to the user's mobile number through an SMS gateway. It then displays a second screen to the user prompting them to enter the OTT. (This is the simple Spring Web Flow customisation we referred to). If the database has the correct mobile number and the user is in possession of the phone at that time, they will receive the OTT as an SMS message and can then enter it at the second screen. CAS will then validate the OTT against the value stored in the database (checking the timestamp to make sure the value isn't stale). If the OTT matches, it means the user has passed the second factor test. CAS then generates its tickets and proceeds to redirect the user's browser back to the application as normal.

The diagram on the following page illustrates the flow of logic.

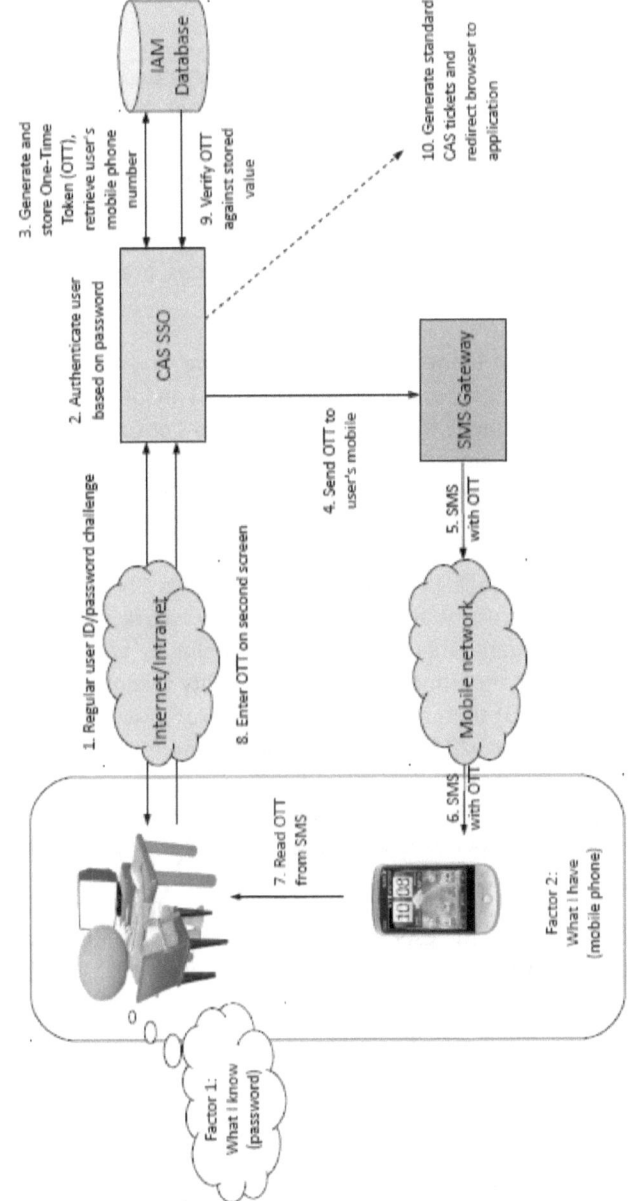

Fig 24: Two-factor authentication

Extension Case Study 3: Federated Identity with SAML Tokens

In theory, it is fairly simple to extend our Two-Layer Protocol Architecture to support federated identity mechanisms as well.

As we mentioned before, the key aspect of federated identity is that the organisation that receives user credentials does not have to have that user previously provisioned within its user directory. The information about the user (a set of assertions) is taken on trust because it is asserted by a trusted partner organisation. For this to happen, we need a way to authenticate the assertions rather than the user. This is usually done by validating a digitally signed document against the signing organisation's public key that has previously been received through a trusted channel.

To understand federated identity systems better, we find it useful to refine the standard model containing a Service Provider (SP) and an Identity Provider (IdP), by identifying a third component that we call an Identity Consumer (IdC). The identity Consumer is just a role played by the Identity Provider itself when the Service Provider requests it to validate a service token, but we find it useful to separate this role out under a separate name, and you will see why shortly.

In the standard CAS model, the CAS SSO server is the one that performs authentication of user credentials against a directory, checks their access rights to the application[28] and generates tickets. At this point in time, it is the Identity Provider, because it is generating one or more identity tokens. The interceptor (on behalf of the application) then receives a service ticket that it is expected to trust. Typically, the interceptor will ask the CAS SSO server to validate the presented ticket before it grants access to the resources it protects. It's a way of asking, "Do you really know this guy?" At this point, the CAS SSO server plays the role of the Identity Consumer, because it is being presented with an identity token that it has to verify.

In the non-federated case, the CAS SSO server is both the Identity Provider and the Identity Consumer and sits within the corporate network.

---

[28] Of course, as described before, the actual *enforcement* of access control may be performed by the interceptor instead of by CAS based on the roles that are (or aren't!) passed in. However, the logical function of validating authorisation is performed by CAS.

Identity Management on a Shoestring

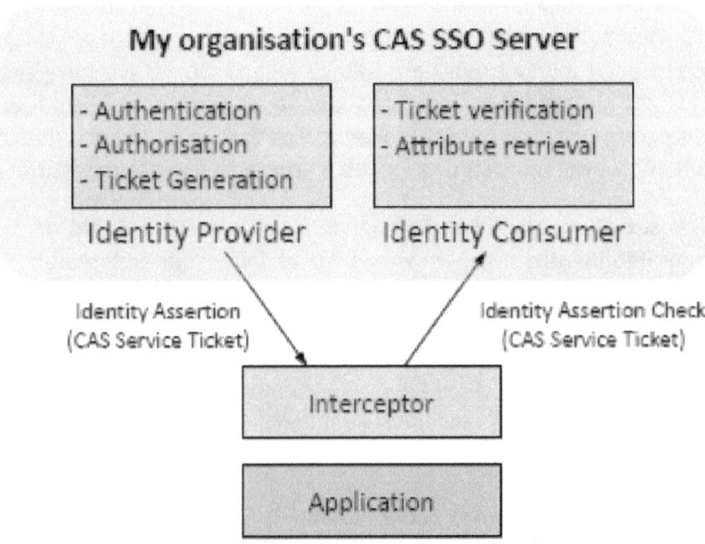

Fig 25: Access Management – Non-federated Model

In the federated case, imagine the two halves of the CAS SSO server being stretched across a network and implemented on opposite sides of the corporate firewall. Let's say the business partner organisation implements the Identity Provider function. Then your organisation must implement the Identity Consumer.

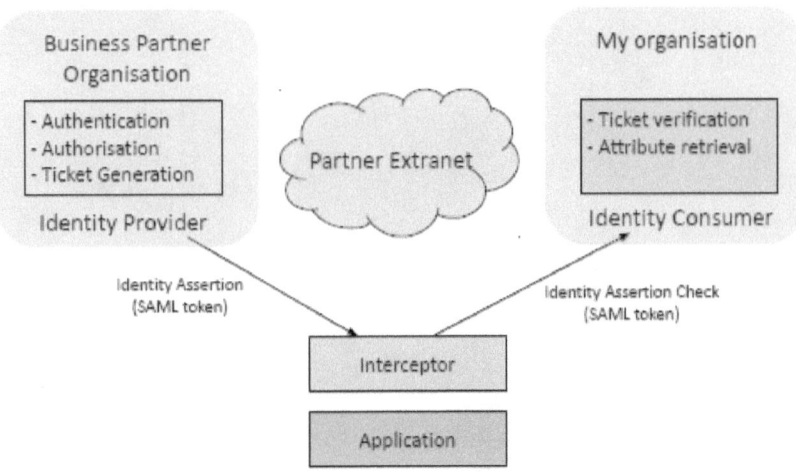

Fig 26: Access Management – Federated Model

Not all organisations use CAS, so we can hardly expect the Identity Assertion to be a CAS Service Ticket. The industry standard for identity assertions is a SAML2[29] token. We therefore need a way to validate SAML2 tokens. But as we have seen, token validation is not all there is to federated identity management. Even if we extend CAS to integrate with a SAML2 token validation component, that's not an architectural fit for the federated case. This is where Shibboleth enters the picture.

Rather than set up a completely independent infrastructure based on Shibboleth for the federated identity case, we would like to follow our architectural approach of using the CAS protocol internally, so that our interceptors do not have to know about Shibboleth. The University of California at Merced has pretty much the same idea, and they provide a Shibboleth-CAS "gateway" to keep interceptors innocent of the existence of Shibboleth. They have a more interesting way to justify the Two-Layer Protocol Architecture. In their eloquent words, it is easier to "CASify" applications than to "Shibbolize" them.

The following diagram shows a setup combining CAS and Shibboleth to provide federated identity using the same pattern as for LAN integration with SPNEGO.

---

[29] Security Assertion Markup Language, a dialect of XML. CAS version 4 is slated to support the SAML2 format even for its own Service Tickets, but the version we used was CAS 3.3.1, which used a native format.

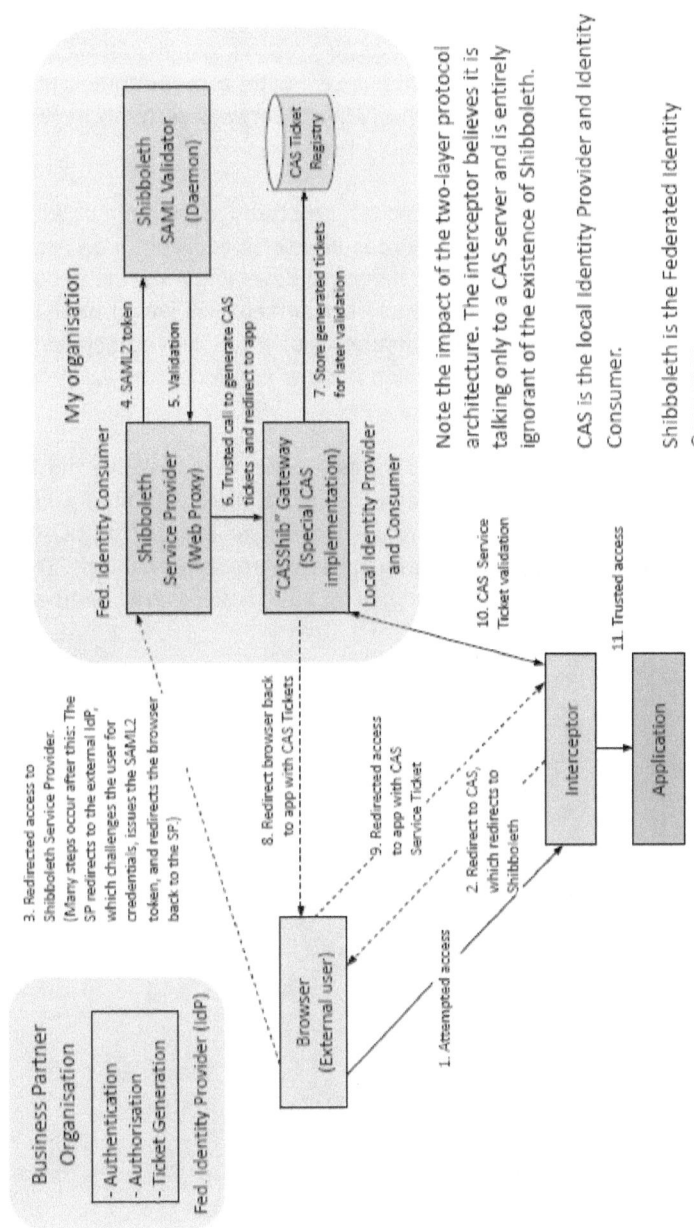

Fig 27: CASShib

Limits to the Two-Layer Protocol Architecture

At first glance, we seem to have managed to preserve our model (i.e., the Two-Layer Protocol Architecture) even when faced with a requirement to support federated identity. The developers of the CASShib Gateway certainly have the right architectural idea.

However, the *implementation* of CASShib lacks maturity at the time of writing. The product and architecture have not been security-certified. More worryingly for its prospects, it has not gathered the critical mass of development activity required for a successful Open Source project, and its development has languished. Therefore we don't believe we can avoid the complexity of a full-fledged Service Provider infrastructure at each business application node where federated identity is to be supported.

A more realistic implementation of federated identity may look like the following diagram. The same application, when accessed by locally-provisioned users as well as by users not locally provisioned, would need to be exposed as two separate domain names (URLs) and protected through two different mechanisms. This model is more complex at each application node, but it has its own overall symmetry when you gaze at it for a while.

Identity Management on a Shoestring

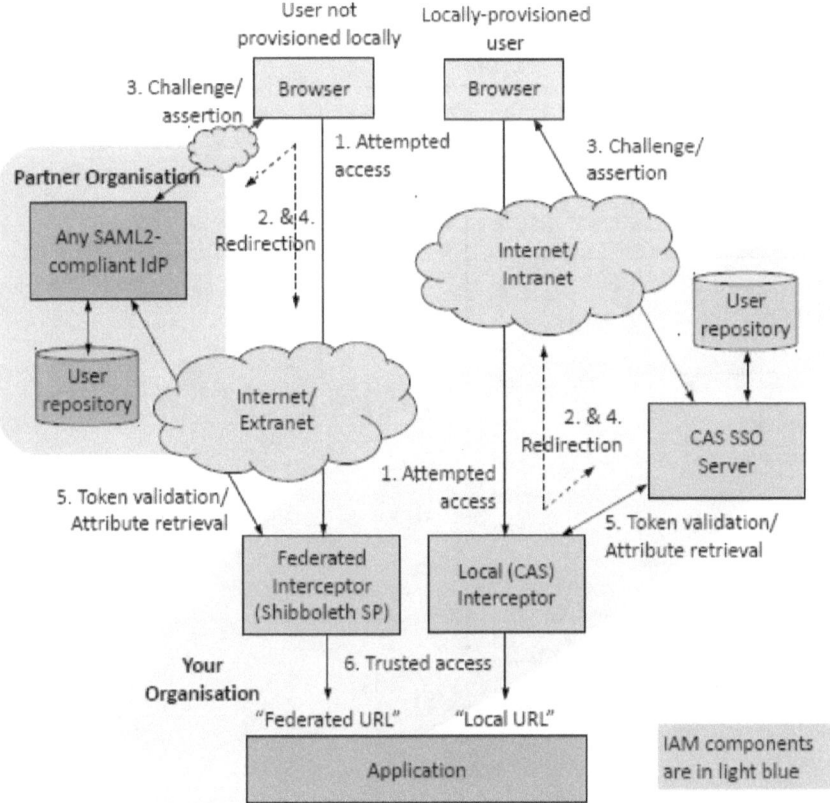

Fig 28: Federated identity – Partner Access to Your Applications

A similar architecture in reverse would apply if your organisation's users had to be granted access to a partner organisation's applications. You would host a Shibboleth IdP backed up by a user repository, and your partner organisation would host some SAML2-compliant SP to protect their application.

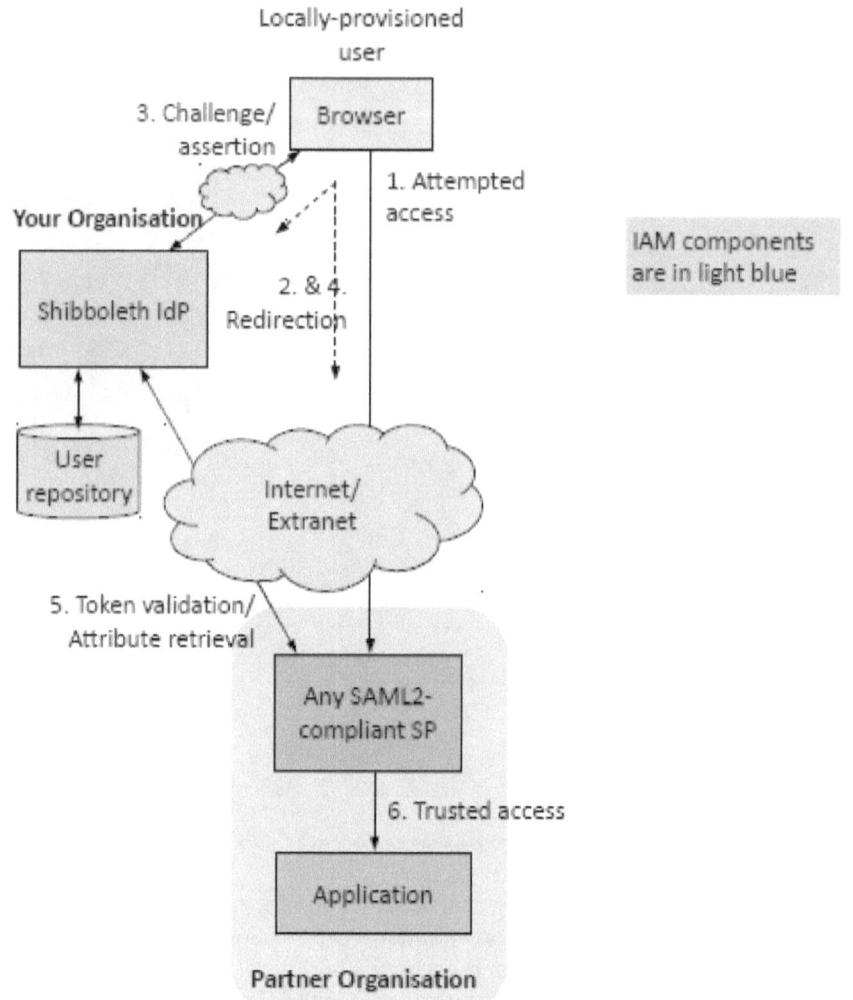

Fig 29: Federated identity – Your Access to Partner Applications

It is important not to confuse a locally-provisioned user with an internal (B2E) user. A locally-provisioned user could be a B2E, B2B or B2C user, but you are responsible for provisioning them in your organisation's user repository. Users who are not provisioned locally are those for whom your partner organisation is responsible. Your partner organisation will vouch for the identity, roles and other attributes of these users. You know nothing about them because they are not found in your user repository. You take all these attributes on trust, because you have the mechanism to verify that it is indeed your trusted partner organisation that is making those assertions.

That should give you a good picture of federated identity and how Shibboleth works. There's a bit of work involved in setting it all up, but hopefully you will see that it's conceptually quite simple. The challenge is to resist the pulls of expediency and to implement a clean design.

Miscellaneous Topics in Access Management

There are a few items we haven't covered in the course of our study of the LIMA Access Management model, so let's do so right away.

Protecting Non-Web Applications

While web applications are the bulk of an organisation's modern fleet of applications, there are important applications built using earlier generations of technologies.

Native Windows-based applications are probably the second-largest group.

Standalone Java applications are probably another significant group. Mainframe-based "green screen" applications are a third set altogether.

And then there are Unix system accounts.

Let's be realistic. We can't provide a seamless IAM "layer" over all these disparate types of applications, but we can come pretty close. Here's how.

Windows-native applications can use SPNEGO directly and transparently authenticate against Active Directory. They'll need to skip coarse-grained authorisation and implement just fine-grained authorisation. This is no real loss of capability or security vulnerability if the fine-grained access control logic is implemented right.

Standalone Java applications have a choice of techniques, because some of them are client-server systems, while others run purely on the client. We recommend building a common security module for the client side of all Java apps, bundled as a jar file with all of them. The CAS classes that authenticate against the IAM directory, perform coarse-grained access control checks against the IAM database and retrieve user attributes from it, should be replicated within a separate server module to serve Java client applications. The client security module should call this server module (over HTTP or RMI) to invoke its services for authentication, coarse-grained authorisation and attribute retrieval. The client-server systems can have a listener on the server side to hook into the IAM User Event Bus to provision users.

The pure client systems can't do this and you will have to explore other mechanisms, some of which may have to be manual. It's a bit of work and unlikely to be 100% satisfactory, but then, it's a different technology and will require effort to harmonise with the rest of the ecosystem. There are smartcard technologies that will allow better integration, such as Sun's Sun Ray system. It depends on how far you want to go to acquire seamless integration and how you define "good enough".

Mainframe "green screen" programs have their own security model (RACF/ACF2). The best that we believe is possible is to hook up the provisioning on the mainframe with IAM's User Event Bus. Having template or model users with canned access rules is a good shortcut for user provisioning, since these can be referenced when creating new users. Access Management will have to be handled entirely by the mainframe.

For Unix system accounts, consider using a Pluggable Authentication Module (PAM) to interface with the IAM directory rather than rely on the local "passwd" and "shadow" files to store user data.

Implementing "Single Sign-Out"

Our experience has shown us that while business units often demand Single Sign-*On* for their users, they don't realise that an unintended consequence is that it no longer makes sense to speak of logging out of any single application. The term "Single Sign-*Out*" is sometimes talked about, but this (if implemented) can be quite irritating from a usability perspective.

Remember that Single Sign-On is defined for *the environment as a whole* and is governed by a single SSO token stored in a cookie on the user's browser. The SSO token is usually valid for many hours, usually a full working day, so that a user does not have to log in again once they have done so at the start of their working day. In contrast, service tickets or application access tokens typically expire after a few minutes, and it is only the validity of an application's web session that governs the need for a user to be revalidated by the SSO server. Logging out of an application in most cases involves invalidating the web session (and perhaps the service ticket), but importantly, *this does not prevent the user from transparently regaining access to the application*.

The reason for this behaviour is that an application interceptor may redirect a user back to the SSO server if the web session or service ticket is no longer valid, but as long as the SSO token is still valid, the user will not be challenged for their login credentials again. After all, this is the required behaviour for SSO. The SSO server will check the user's access rights against the IAM database and as long as the access is still granted, will *silently* generate a fresh service ticket which will let the user into the application once more.

The effect of this is that a user cannot be logged out of any application as long as their SSO session is valid. This comes as a bit of a shock to business owners and even some security people because it implies that an open browser can be used by any passer-by to gain access to sensitive applications, even if the legitimate user has "logged out" of them and closed the relevant browser tabs.

Note that while this behaviour is definitely less secure than what we had with standalone applications, it is not a bug or a drawback with IAM or with Single Sign-On, merely a failure to understand the implications of the Single Sign-On feature that is otherwise desired.

A common knee-jerk response to this security problem is to demand implementation of "Single Sign-Out". In effect, the global login session is to be terminated when the user finishes up with the individual business application in question. Indeed, CAS has a simple mechanism to invalidate the SSO token, so

"Single Sign-Out" is very easy to implement. However, this sledgehammer approach is quite a nuisance, because the user will then have to log in again to access any other application. Single Sign-Out negates the benefits of Single Sign-On! We may as well have stayed with standalone applications and just used a centralised user directory for authentication and authorisation.

We believe that the most pragmatic approach is to rely on old-fashioned workstation timeouts at the operating system level to lock the user's workstation itself after a certain period of inactivity. This narrows the window available for opportunistic access to passers-by. It is also the generic solution to protect applications, because it is in any case impossible to enforce a rule that users must log out of sensitive applications before leaving their workstations.

A combination of workstation timeouts and education about the implications of Single Sign-On is the most practical solution to this security issue.

IAM and Cloud Computing

When Yoda said, "Clouded our vision was," he did so ruefully. But today, the vision for any software system must include the Cloud!

For end-user organisations that rely on Infrastructure as a Service (IaaS) clouds, IAM is something they would need to set up themselves to protect the applications they upload to it[30].

Cloud providers who offer a Platform as a Service (PaaS) need to worry about setting up a supporting set of shared services on top of a basic IaaS for client applications that are deployed on their platform, and IAM is a classic shared service that they would need to configure[31].

Both groups of people need to understand how IAM plays in the cloud.

One may be tempted to ask, "Is CAS or Shibboleth the better product for the Cloud?"

The question, however, is misguided. The important factor to consider is where users are provisioned relative to where the applications they access are hosted.

- If the user repository is hosted on the same cloud that hosts the applications those users access, then this is a case of local identity management, and CAS will do nicely.

- If the user repository and the applications that users access are hosted on different clouds, then this is a case of federated identity management, and Shibboleth is the better fit.

The following diagram illustrates this rule with the help of a mnemonic.

C: Co-located user repository and applications – use CAS
S: Separately located user repository and applications – use Shibboleth

---

[30] End-users of Platform as a Service (PaaS) clouds don't have to worry about designing IAM configurations. They would just use the IAM-equivalent services provided by their vendor. The design of IAM is even less relevant for end-users of Software as a Service (SaaS) platforms.

[31] E.g., Amazon Web Services include IAM, which is leveraged in their Beanstalk PaaS offering.

Identity Management on a Shoestring

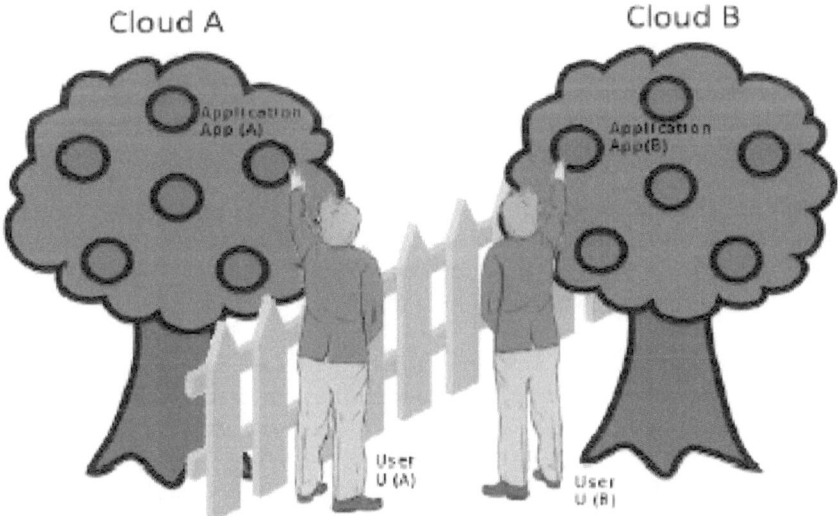

Fig 30: Cloud and User Repository Location

The term "cloud" should not faze us. These are all distributed systems with the same underlying principles. And as we said before, don't confuse locally-provisioned users with internal (B2E) users.

What Do We Do with Active Directory?

We've talked about the IAM directory and we'll shortly show how minimal its data structure really is. However, most organisations with Windows workstations also have Active Directory to provide a centralised authentication point for LAN logins, as we saw during our SPNEGO discussion.

Can organisations use AD as their IAM directory? This may seem trivial to do, but there are some organisational reasons why it may not be a good idea. The more elegant solution, we believe, is to maintain *both* directories. This may appear logistically more complex, but doesn't have to be.

AD has a fairly complex data structure, and it holds data on many entities (e.g., workstations and printers) in addition to users. The temptation when using AD as the IAM directory is to go the whole hog and do away with the IAM database altogether. That would be a bad idea. The separation of directory and database, loosely coupled by the User UUID, is one of the biggest effort-saving innovations we have seen. In fact, we would recommend using as many directories as required to authenticate different groups of users, but to share a single IAM database for their authorisation[32]. Directories should hold authentication credentials and nothing else. As always, the UUID is the link between repositories that reconciles user data between any directory and the database. (A trivial format conversion may be required between AD's GUID and IAM's UUID[33].)

---

[32] The UUID's role in decoupling authentication and authorisation realms is illustrated diagrammatically later on.

[33] The curly brace-delimited GUID "{0fec5f441dc64b4e8dd0a5404520118d}" favoured by Microsoft corresponds to the hyphenated UUID format "0fec5f44-1dc6-4b4e-8dd0-a5404520118d" that is more common in the Unix world.

Identity Management on a Shoestring

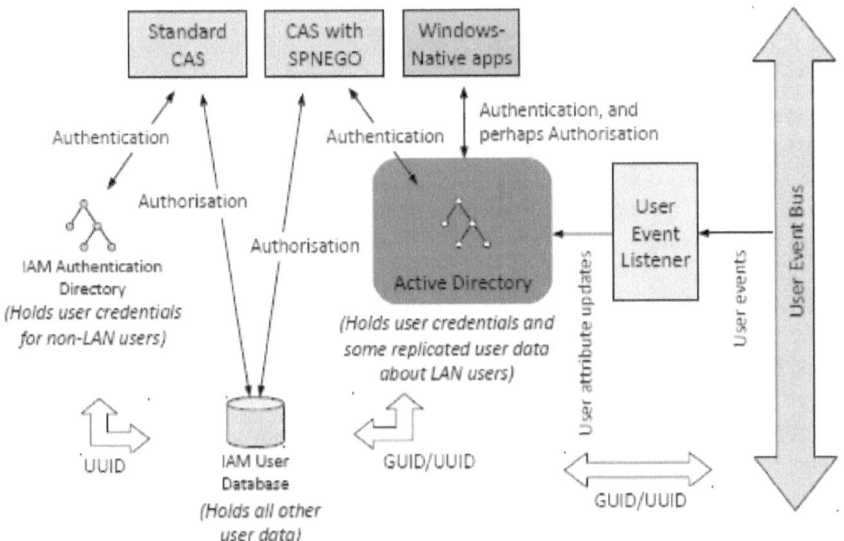

Fig 31: How to Incorporate Active Directory into an IAM System

If other (Windows-native) applications require AD to store some user information that they rely on, then treat AD as an "Associated System" in IAM that holds replicated user data, and implement a listener on the User Event Bus to update those user attributes when they change within IAM.

The above diagram summarises our recommendation.

Tailoring Coarse-Grained Access Control

As we have seen, CAS can retrieve user attributes from the IAM database right after the very first authentication in an SSO session and store them in the Ticket Registry along with the Ticket-Granting Ticket. This provides a performance optimisation because it then doesn't have to go back to the IAM database to retrieve them every time a new application is accessed during that SSO session. The Ticket Registry is always accessed for ticket validation in any case, so an extra database access thereby avoided.

You may find though, that a generic set of user attributes is not good enough to enforce application-specific access control. Even if IAM restricts itself to coarse-grained access control, we may implement it through a mapping from the user to an application role such as "Application X User". We may also need to pass other attributes that are specific to each application, such as local user IDs on associated systems that that particular application may have to access.

At the cost of a slight performance penalty, we can extend CAS's default functionality to make an extra database retrieval once ticket validation is over, and add an application-specific set of attributes to the generic ones that are stored with the TGT.

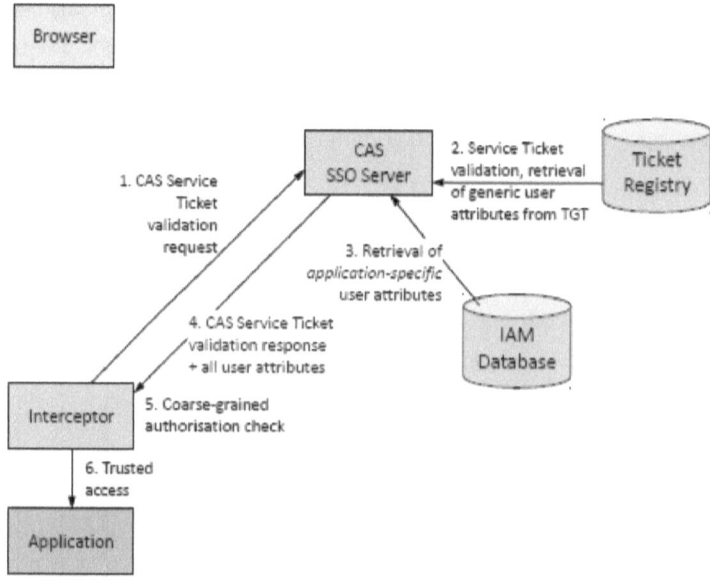

Fig 32: Coarse-grained access control

We now have a means of enforcing coarse-grained access control through IAM. If the interceptor does not find the specific attribute it is looking for, it means the user is not authorised to access the application. It can then either display a suitable error message, or it can pass the request through to the application (with the expected attribute missing), so that the application can perform a similar check and provide a gracefully degraded level of functionality (e.g., "guest" access).

Using CAS to Centralise Enforcement of Authorisation Rules

One idea that occurred to us was to ask why CAS could not perform a coarse-grained authorisation check against the IAM database right after the authentication check against the IAM directory. Wouldn't that be more guaranteeably secure from an auditor's perspective than just passing back user attributes and leaving enforcement to each application's interceptor?

In other words, how about a process as shown below, where CAS actively *blocks* access if step 7 fails?

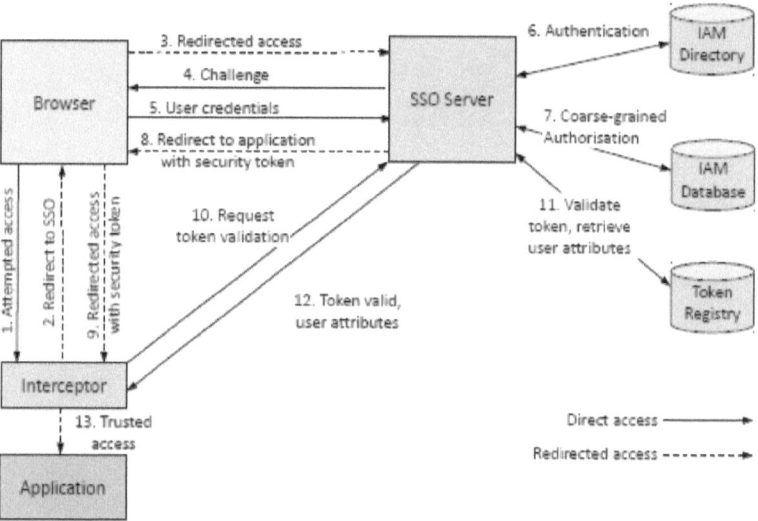

Fig 33: Centralised enforcement

Well, even though CAS has historically been an authentication mechanism for distributed systems and not really an authorisation system, it is after all an Open Source product, so it can be modified to perform this function with very little effort.

When we explored this design option however, we encountered some usability concerns that neutralised its minor edge in auditability. These issues could be fairly universal, so you should think about them too.

What should CAS do if a user is correctly authenticated but doesn't have access rights to the application they are trying to access? Should it just display an error page?

Application owners typically want control over the look-and-feel of error pages, especially when delivering sensitive news like a denial of access. They may want to sugar-coat the pill in different ways. While it is possible to tailor CAS's functionality to show different error screens for different applications, we are now straying a fair bit away from enterprise functionality and into application territory. It's better to let application owners themselves design (and re-design!) their error pages.

Also, some applications prefer to degrade the access level to "guest" privileges when authorisation fails. For these reasons, we decided to stick to the approach of using the interceptor to enforce tailored access control. You could of course, implement the above logic if it works for you.

Using a Reverse-Proxy Device as a Common Interceptor

Another approach we considered was to centralise the interception function through a reverse-proxy that is set up to intercept access to all web applications in the network. This has several architectural advantages, the most important being its guarantee of protection to all applications in the network at a single stroke. While software-based proxies face concerns of being potential performance bottlenecks, there is a class of hardware devices that are quite performant and effective in this role.

The diagram below illustrates how a reverse proxy device could work as a common interceptor.

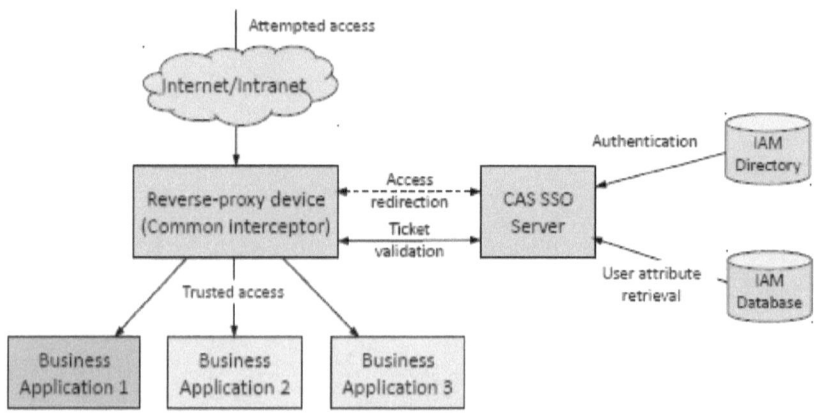

Fig 34: Reverse proxy

However, we faced two problems with this design, a minor one and a major one.

The minor problem was that very few of the devices we surveyed had support for the CAS protocol. A couple had support for Kerberos, which would also have been acceptable. However, the programming models were quite limited and could have constrained the development of customised logic, which was a definite requirement.

This constraint could also have been worked around, but in any case, the major problem that stymied this approach was cost, specifically the initial outlay required.

A reverse-proxy device of the required capability and acceptable quality costs about $100,000 at the time of writing. We would have had to deploy this in a redundant, load-balanced configuration for availability if not scalability. That meant a minimum of two devices in the production environment. But any medium-to-large organisation has a number of environments in which its applications are deployed, i.e., development, system testing, user acceptance testing (UAT), production and disaster recovery (DR). We would have needed one device in the development environment and two each in the others, bringing the total number of devices to 9. A single device costing $100,000 really meant a cost outlay of almost a million dollars for the overall solution.

So while the architectural model was quite elegant and the purchase was well worth the price from an enterprise viewpoint, the usual budgetary constraints ensured that this approach never got off the ground. You should however consider this model if you can manage the initial outlay.

Access Management for "Portal" Applications

Many organisations have "portals", which are gateways that aggregate and provide a common point of access to a group of business applications. IAM is expected to provide security for portals as well. It's important to realise that there is a portal *function* that is different from a specialised model that is portal *technology*.

The portal function is a simple one of providing some form of aggregation, so that a user sees all their required functions in the same place and they can follow links from that starting point to do those specialised tasks. Many so-called "portals" are nothing but menu pages on websites that provide simple hyperlinks to other full-fledged web applications.

Portal technology, on the other hand, refers to a programming model defined by two Java standards, – JSR-168 and JSR-286. Business functions cannot be standalone web applications in this model. To be able to run inside a portal, they must be written as specialised components called *portlets*. Among other peculiar requirements, portlets must emit fragments of HTML instead of complete web pages and conform to a complex, multi-phase event behaviour defined by these standards. There is also an adjunct standard called WSRP (Web Services for Remote Portlets) that allows portlets and portals of different technology families (i.e., Java and .NET) to interoperate.

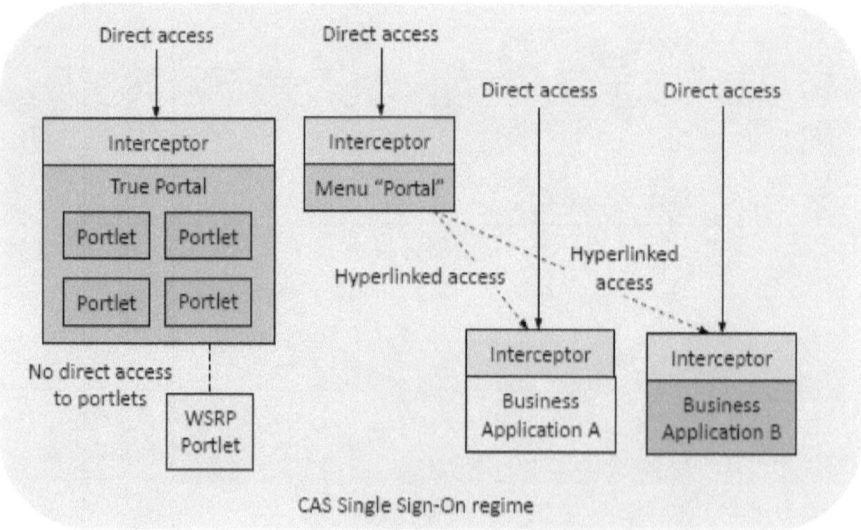

Fig 35: Portals and IAM

The figure above shows what it would look like to integrate portals with IAM.

IAM can protect both types of portals under its SSO regime. The main difference is that a true portal (i.e., the JSR-168/286 and WSRP kind) is seen as a single application. "Menu page" portals and the applications they aggregate are seen as independent web applications at the same level. Here, the portal page is just a convenience for novice users. Advanced users can bookmark and directly access the business applications behind it. With the "true portal" model, access to an individual portlet is not even possible, because portlets only run within the portal environment.

Identity Management, LIMA-style

We've seen how Access Management works. Identity Management is the other half of IAM. We can think of Identity Management as the system that provides Access Management with up-to-date data to work with. It also performs an audit function by keeping track of all significant user events.

Doing all of this behind-the-scenes stuff is hard work. It's conceptually simple, but operationally hard – until you get the processes in place. Then it's both simple and easy. But you need to avoid the expedient shortcuts that can complicate matters over the long run and end up costing you more. The key principle is loose coupling, as always.

Identity Management Concepts

The key processes in Identity Management are User Provisioning and Audit. In essence, User Provisioning is keeping user data up-to-date and consistent on a number of different systems, so that Access Management and Audit can both work correctly. Audit is recording all relevant user events and activities. This diagram puts all these concepts into context.

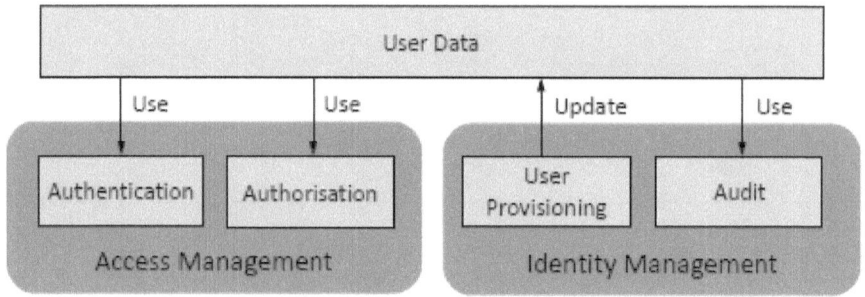

Fig 36: Identity Management concepts

We've already covered many techniques of loose coupling early on. Now is the time to drill down into the details to see what loose coupling really means in the context of Identity Management.

Separating Church and State – The Roles of Directory and Database

If you follow no other recommendation in this document but this one, you will still save yourself hundreds of thousands of dollars of unnecessary effort. It is simply this – split your user data into an LDAP-based directory and a relational database, with only authentication credentials in the directory and everything else in the database. There were many occasions when we had to implement a new feature and thought to ourselves, "Thank goodness we chose to split the user data!" This is such a fundamental design characteristic of a flexible IAM.

A directory server is a strange beast. It evolved at a time when relational databases were being tuned for mixed read-update loads and were not fast enough for read-mostly use cases. Directories emerged to cater to this need. Directory servers were very fast on reads but very slow on updates. This was OK for situations that required lookups much more frequently than updates.

However, in recent times, relational databases have become extremely fast for any kind of load, so performance is no longer a differentiator. On the contrary, the tree structure of a directory is needlessly constraining when you have to model all sorts of complex data relationships. Many data elements in an IAM have a many-to-many relationship[34], and directories simply suck at modelling anything but one-to-one and one-to-many relationships. For example, if you're trying to put user role information into a directory, be warned that you're stepping into quicksand. You will be tearing your hair out very soon. Relational databases are a much better fit for all such information.

You may wonder then why we don't put all our data into a relational database. Is a directory useful at all any more? The short answer is yes. Directories still do certain things extremely well:

- They are good at storing passwords in a secure encrypted form and performing password validations internally with a single operation. Implementing this functionality in a generic relational database will require the application to perform encryption and/or decryption in memory and perform retrievals and comparisons as separate operations. Subsequent functions like recording the

---

[34] Association tables are usually employed to split many-to-many relationships into two one-to-many relationships back-to-back, but they're still hard to fit into a tree-structured data store.

number of failed attempts, or clearing that count on a subsequent successful login, will also have to be explicitly coded.

- Directories can enforce enterprise password policies based on simple configuration settings. Aspects of security policy such as password length, password expiry (i.e., how frequently must passwords be changed?), password history (e.g., users cannot reuse the last 15 passwords), invalid logins allowed (i.e., how many times can a user enter incorrect credentials before the account gets locked?), etc., are very easy to specify in a directory[35]. A general purpose database needs special application logic to enforce these aspects of security policy.

---

[35] Some aspects of password policy (e.g., a password must contain at least one uppercase letter, one lowercase letter and a digit) may still require to be specified at the application level, especially since it is considered more user-friendly for an application to provide a continuous indication of password acceptability as the user is typing.

Identity Management on a Shoestring

Designing the IAM Directory

Tip 1: As mentioned before, your directory should contain only user IDs and passwords as core data, with a couple of other attributes we will cover in a moment. You may organise user records under different organisation units (e.g., "ou=internal, ou=users"), but the user object itself should have no other attributes, not even the user's name or type (B2B, B2C, etc.) It may seem unnatural to have such a minimal directory structure, but resist the temptation to put in anything more, and you will be thankful for this restraint on many future occasions.

This is a minimal structure for the user node of the directory that will serve you well:

Fig 37: A minimal directory structure

Tip 2: The larger structure that caters for internal and external users may look like this:

Fig 38: A more comprehensive directory structure

Tip 3: Although you may split B2E and B2C users into separate sub-trees, it may not be possible to do so with B2B and B2B2C users.

This is because B2B2C users are customers of your business partners, and you may have a common external-facing portal for both these types of users to log into. In these cases, you won't actually know which kind of user they are at the moment they hit your portal's login page and enter their credentials, and so binding to the right sub-tree of the directory for authentication will be a challenge. It's far better to treat all external users the same as far as placing them in the directory goes. You can of course tell whether they're B2B or B2B2C after authentication, because the "user type" attribute is in the database.

Tip 4: The last point implies that we need a way to map the user record in the directory to the corresponding one in the database. The attribute that provides this mapping is what we call a "User UUID". This is a random, meaning-free and universally unique identifier that you can confidently use without fear of conflict with any previously assigned identifier[36]. This is what you will use to map a user record in the directory to the corresponding record in the relational database (see figure below).

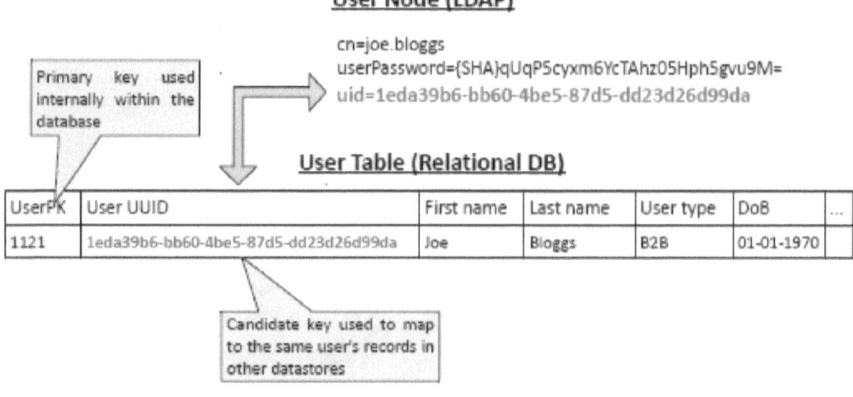

Fig 39: Mapping directory to database

---

[36] A UUID is a 128-bit string, and the chances of two randomly generated UUIDs being the same is about 1 in 10^{33}. These are such stupendous odds (and modern pseudo-random number generation algorithms so reliable), that you can blindly insert records in a table without checking for duplicates. If someone you know insists that you must check for duplicate UUIDs before inserting new records, they probably don't understand how big a number 10^{33} really is, and are probably disappointed that the Universe has "only" 10^{80} atoms! The authors have learnt not to argue in such situations.

As part of its Access Management function, CAS will authenticate the user's credentials (cn and userPassword values) against the directory, then use the uid (User UUID) attribute of the directory user object to retrieve any other required attributes of the user from the relational database[37].

Tip 5: Try and implement password policies at a per-user level

Your organisation's security policy may specify different rules governing passwords for B2E users, B2B users and B2C/B2B2C users[38]. Most directories only support password policies at an "ou" node level (which then affects user nodes below that root node), but as we have seen above, sometimes we are forced to place B2B and B2B2C users under the same "ou" sub-tree, in which case this approach to password policies wouldn't work. It has to be more fine-grained. We need a reference to the applicable password policy to be stored at the level of the user node, not a parent node. OpenLDAP is one of the few directory servers that implement this feature.

Tip 6: Have a separate sub-tree for "system" objects

The reference to the password policy node in the user nodes above hints at a separate system sub-tree. Here is where you may want to store password policies as well as "system accounts" (i.e., directory administrator accounts as well as user IDs corresponding to applications rather than to human users). The structure of this part of the tree may look like this:

---

[37] The query may require a SQL join to map the User UUID to the primary key used within the relational database, because tables within the database only reference the local primary key.
[38] Internal users may need to change their passwords every month, while customers may be allowed to keep theirs for 3 months. Internal users may not be allowed to reuse the last 10 passwords, while customers may not have such a restriction, etc.

Fig 40: System objects in the directory structure

User UUID – The One Ring to Rule Them All

The User UUID as the association between user records in the authentication directory and the user database is a generic pattern you should try to use when associating user records across any two systems. The User UUID should be a candidate key in every application or system where user provisioning is in some way to be managed by the IAM (what we call "Associated Systems"), but it need not be the primary key in any of them. In fact, we recommend that you always use another local primary key in each system, in the interests of loose coupling. However, many legacy systems will be unable to support a local mapping to the User UUID. In such cases, the IAM database will need to hold that mapping for them.

The diagram below shows both mechanisms of mapping user identity across systems. The UUID-based mapping is preferred, and the Associated System table is the fallback when this is not feasible.

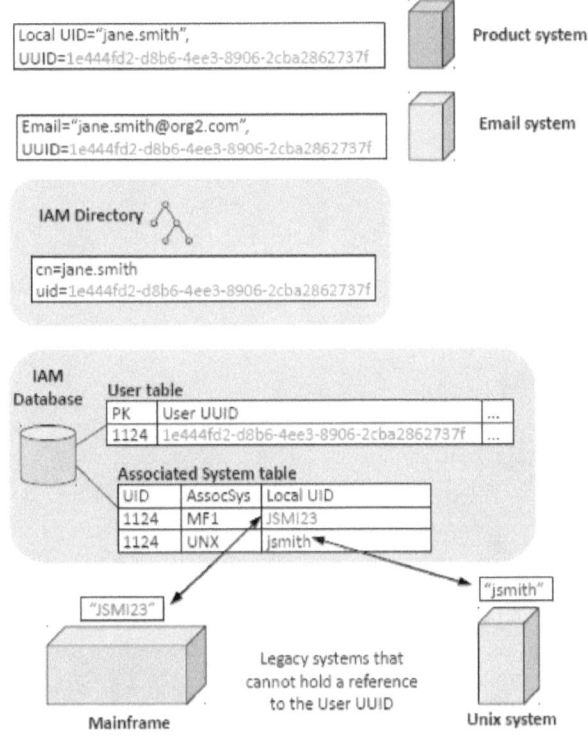

Fig 41: The User UUID as the link between systems

Ganesh Prasad and Umesh Rajbhandari

Decoupling Authentication, Coarse-grained and Fine-grained Authorisation Realms

The following diagram shows how the consistent use of a User UUID makes it easy to manage the Authentication and Authorisation requirements of different (even overlapping) groups of users with absolute flexibility in the choice of products at each level. (Of course, if an associated system cannot hold a UUID reference, then the IAM database must hold the mapping.)

Identity Management on a Shoestring

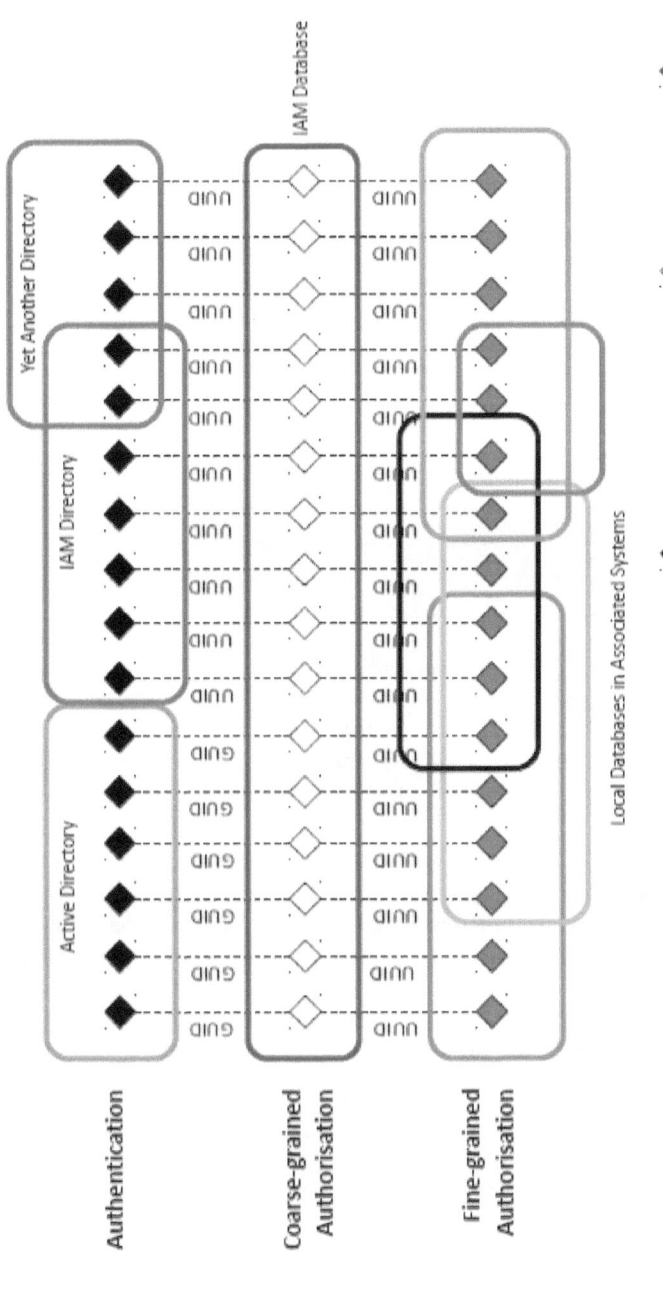

Fig 42: Decoupling realms

Person UUID – The Ultimate Identity Reference

Associating various system accounts through a common identity at the user level (i.e., a User UUID) is definitely a convenient handle for user administration across applications and systems at a point in time.

However, another very common requirement is an audit query that seeks to associate the actions of a person at various points in time, and this may span multiple engagements of the person under different user identities. What we need is a simple, unobtrusive method that can be applied at any time to create this extra level of association.

We suggest creating a "Person UUID" that can be used to map to multiple "User UUID" values, as shown below:

Person UUID	User UUID	Updated by	Timestamp
02a6d45c-a516-42a5-848f-90070b1a5c1b	a55ad891-de39-4e1a-9cb1-c898fc9be9e8	1033	...
02a6d45c-a516-42a5-848f-90070b1a5c1b	1e444fd2-d8b6-4ee3-8906-2cba2862737f	1033	...
...	...	...	...

Table 1: Person UUID mapping table

This is a one-to-many mapping that sits "outside" of the rest of the IAM database, so to speak. This mapping can be created whenever a relationship between two users is discovered through some out-of-band mechanism (say, through a name or address search).

The Person UUID will have no attributes of its own, because attributes are generally captured at the User level. You may need some conventions to report on Persons, perhaps using the attributes of the most recent User associated with the Person.

The following diagram illustrates the use of both the Person UUID and the User UUID as handles to manage user information.

Person, User and System Account – A Flexible Mapping Scheme

Scenario: In 2008, Jane Doe was a B2B user (employee of a business partner) who was granted access to several of our company's systems. By 2010, she had married and changed her name to Jane Smith. She also changed jobs. She was once again granted access to these same systems as a fresh B2B user through her new employer.

- As of 2008 (or 2010), how can we manage all of Jane's system accesses together in a convenient and consistent way?
- How can we answer an audit query whether something Jane did in 2010 relates to something she did in 2008 as part of her earlier engagement?

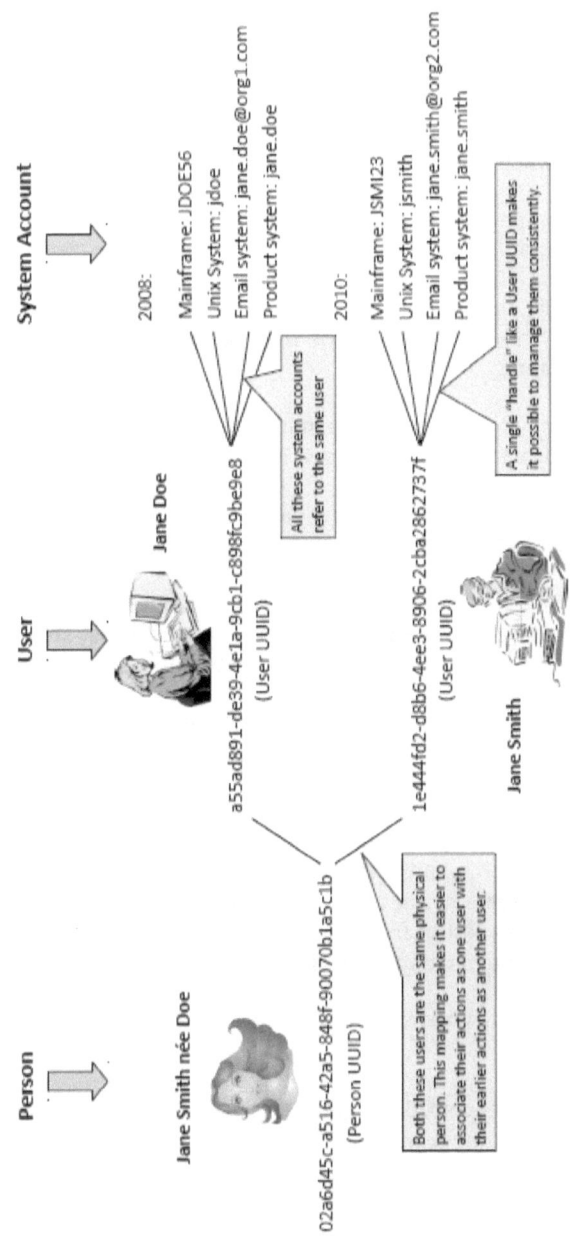

Fig 43: The Person UUID as the link between various user incarnations of the same physical person

Data Replication and Master Data Management

One of the common mistakes possible when implementing an IAM system is to duplicate information across more than one repository, with an excessive reliance on product-based replication mechanisms to keep them in sync. This is highly error-prone in practice and will be a perennial source of maintenance headaches.

Our recommendation is to stick to well-understood principles of Master Data Management (MDM):

- Identify the application or system that is the "source of truth" for each data item. This system should be the only one that creates, updates or deletes this data item.

- Try and store each data item in only one place. The most natural place to store it is local to the system that is its "source of truth".

- Try to avoid replicas of any data item. If possible, let other systems that need access to this data item query it directly from the source of truth.

- If it is too cumbersome or it creates unnecessary dependencies to force such queries back to the source of truth, then consider storing a read-only replica of the data item locally with some strict rules around its management.

- Needless to say, read-only copies of data items must never be updated locally. They can only be periodically refreshed from the source of truth.

In an ideal world, all systems that store user data will maintain a "User UUID" candidate key into each user record. This will be used as a reference key whenever a source of truth for any user attribute wants to propagate updates to that attribute to all other systems that may maintain a copy of it[39]. When we talk about User Provisioning as part of the Identity Management capability of IAM, we will describe how this can be made to work elegantly.

A good (if somewhat complex) discussion on Master Data Management can be found here:

http://www.ibm.com/developerworks/data/library/techarticle/dm-0804oberhofer/index.html

---

[39] For systems that cannot hold a UUID reference, the IAM Associated System table will provide the local user ID as the key to be used by that associated system for performing these updates.

Designing the IAM Database

It may seem a daunting task to design a custom database for your organisation's requirements, but hopefully, the following tips and suggestions will make the job easier.

Tip 1: Keep core tables minimal and store sets of related attributes in other tables

Normally, the tendency is to store all attributes that have a one-to-one relationship with an entity's primary key together in one table. We have found that it is more flexible to group such attributes and store them in separate tables.

For example, the user table should have very few attributes in it. The user's name should be stored in a separate table with the related attributes of title, first name, last name, preferred name, etc. Sometimes, it may be required to store details of users for whom such information doesn't make sense, for example system or admin accounts. Decoupling attributes in this way avoids having to carry null values when they are meaningless.

Another example is the "application" table. Keep this minimal (just code and description), and hold other attributes like URLs to be protected in another table.

Tip 2: Make the UUID a candidate key of the User table

Design the IAM database as you would any other application, i.e., the primary key of the user table is a database-internal field, perhaps an automatically-generated sequence number. This value will hence be the foreign key in other tables that reference the user. The UUID needs to be a candidate key in the User table, and that should be the logical entry point from other systems. A simple join spanning the UUID and the User table's primary key will allow you to access any user attribute, so this is a trivial indirection. It's needlessly cumbersome to make the UUID the primary key.

Tip 3: Consider application-specific roles rather than global roles

We haven't found much value in defining global (i.e., organisation-wide) roles. What we think are relevant are global role names or role types. These are standard identifiers such as "Administrator", "User" and "Read-Only User". You can have codes and descriptions for each. Where these are useful is when they are combined with applications. For example, if the IAM protects an ERP system and an HR system, then we may have 6 "application roles" in all (ERP Administrator, ERP User,

ERP Read-Only User, HR Administrator, HR User and HR Read-Only User). These are the roles that will be granted access to applications. Two role types that are useful for IAM in particular are "Requester" and "Authoriser". Auditors like to ensure that user management functions are initiated (requested) by one user and authorised by another.

Tip 4: Build support for coarse-grained access control, not fine-grained

When stakeholders hear that you are building an IAM, there will be pressure on you to incorporate support for everything they can think of, including the proverbial kitchen sink. One of the really insidious requirements is fine-grained access control. An example of this is the expectation that IAM will control the specific screens and buttons that a user can access within an application. But, looking ahead to the day IAM protects a dozen or more applications, each with its specialised roles and functions, it is clearly a very complex undertaking to try and hold all those various application-specific roles and functions and map the allowed accesses within tables of the IAM database. It gets even worse because applications change their local roles and functions fairly frequently, so IAM will end up having to stay current with the requirements of every application in the ecosystem. This is a largely infeasible task, and allowing fine-grained access control to be part of IAM is asking for trouble. Resist such pressure strongly. IAM cannot manage fine-grained function or data access. The most it can do is protect applications themselves as coarse-grained units from unauthorised access. It can also pass in user attributes to these applications as part of the initial access, so applications are free to apply more fine-grained access control logic internally.

Getting the granularity of Role-Based Access Control right is one of the crucial decisions in determining the success of IAM[40].

Tip 5: Understand the difference between "protected applications" and "associated systems"

---

[40] Some companies have a more sophisticated HR practice that defines an enterprise-wide "Job Family Framework" or JFF. If an organisation has no more than 50-100 generic roles that are mapped to specific job titles in individual divisions and departments, then it becomes feasible for IAM to manage this reasonable number of generic roles in its own database. It may be possible to extend the authorisation logic of IAM to include a rules engine that considers the user's JFF role and their department to arrive at more refined judgements of access rights to business functions. In the absence of a JFF, we recommend that IAM stick to coarse-grained roles (I.e,. whether allowed to access an application or not) and leave the individual applications to enforce finer-grained access control logic.

They're both business applications, but "protected applications" in the IAM context are those that have an exposed URL protected by IAM. "Associated systems" are those that have users provisioned in them. So "protected application" is an Access Management concept, while "associated system" is an Identity Management concept. You need separate tables to hold their attributes and the different relationships they have with users. Needless to say, some systems may be both protected applications and associated systems.

Tip 6: Consider maintaining a set of "Associated Roles" for a given role, to automatically cascade role assignment

Sometimes, one application role implies another one. It may be that an Administrator role within a B2B application implies a Requester role within the IAM user management application, because such a user tends to request the creation of other users. Holding such associations in another table can remove the need to remember these role dependencies by automatically cascading them. When a user is assigned one application role, the system can derive the other application roles that must also be assigned, and do the assignment transparently. Of course, revocation of roles must also follow the same logic.

Given a two-step request/authorise workflow, you will need to think about whether to cascade role assignment requests and show all the resulting role assignments as pending changes to an authoriser, or whether to create only the main role assignment request at first and create the other role assignments once this has been approved by the authoriser.

The Associated Roles functionality can be a labour-saving enhancement to the IAM system that is funded separately when the workload justifies it.

Tip 7: Consider using "Role Profiles" as a shorthand to assign a set of application roles that usually go together

Here's an alternative approach to associating roles with each other, so you may only need one or the other scheme.

A corollary of having application-specific coarse-grained roles is that groups of users tend to require similar sets of roles. For example, every customer service representative may need to be granted a "User" role on the corporate intranet (like any other employee), the CRM system and one or more product systems. This set of roles (i.e., "Intranet User", "CRM System User", "Product System X User", etc.) is used repeatedly for so many people that it may make sense to group them into a "Role Profile" as a sort of shorthand and use that in the User Administration screens to quickly assign a set of roles to each new user. Under the covers, the association of each user is still to the different individual roles, so exceptions can be catered for quite easily by dropping or granting additional application roles to individuals.

As before, the association of application-specific roles to "Role Profiles" would be a separate table in the IAM database and can be a later enhancement when patterns of access begin to be established.

Tip 8: Have a table of security questions and another table of per-user answers to two or three of these security questions.

Security questions like "What is your mother's maiden name?" or "What was the name of your first pet?" are alternate ways to identify a user and therefore very useful for providing self-service password reset or forgotten password capability. If a user claims to have forgotten their password, they should enter their user ID. IAM should retrieve their User UUID from the directory using this User ID, then retrieve and display their security questions from the database using the User UUID. If the user is able to answer all the required security questions correctly, a new password should be generated and sent to the user's email address. This password should also be updated in the directory and simultaneously marked "expired", so the user will be forced to reset it on first login.

Tip 9: You will almost certainly need a user activity log

From an audit perspective, many user activities like logins, failed logins, password changes, application accesses, etc., will need to be logged. A separate table will need to record these events.

As this discussion shows, the IAM database can be built up incrementally like all the other components of IAM, so it doesn't have to be developed in a "Big Bang" fashion with an immediate price-tag. The design lends itself to incremental enhancement through layering of functionality, and this is one of its big advantages when project budgets are tight.

The following diagram provides some hints on the types of entities you may need to model, and their likely relationships. You may need about 20-25 tables, which isn't overly complex.

Identity Management on a Shoestring

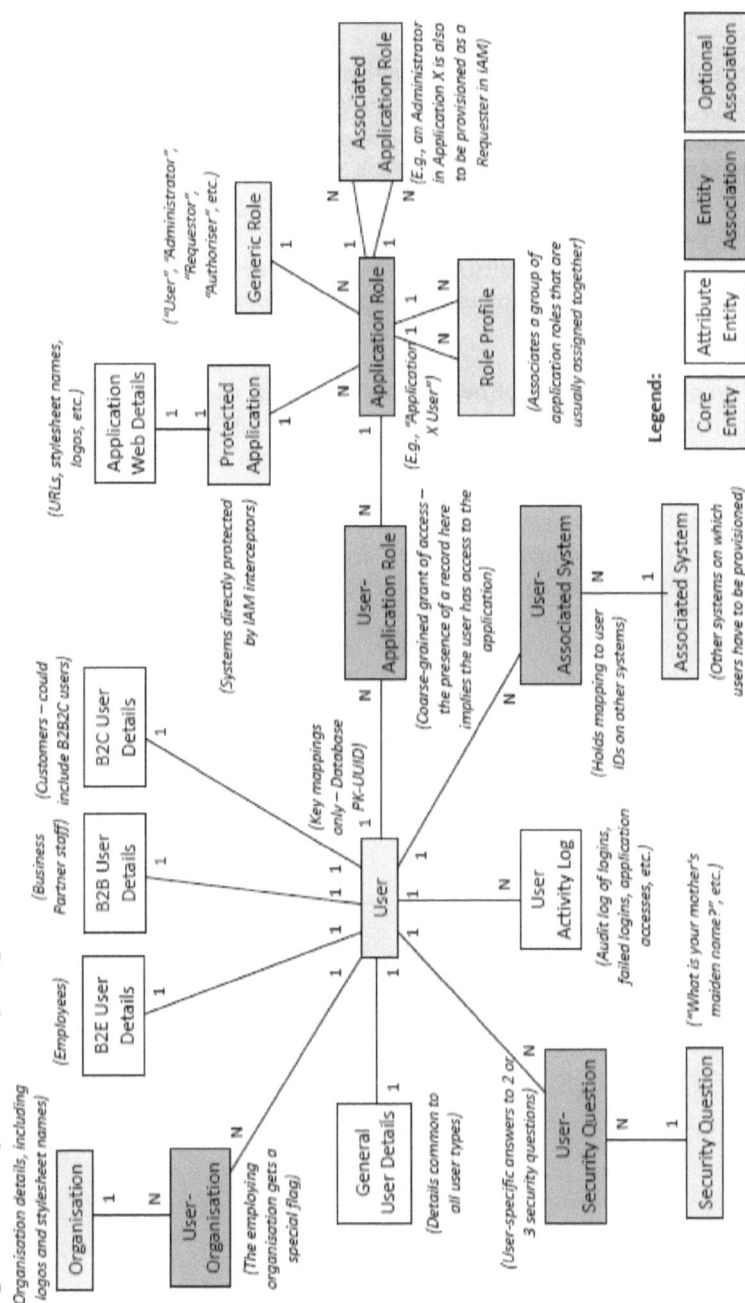

Fig 44: Entity-Relationship Diagram for the IAM database

Tip 9: Use database triggers to record changes to sensitive tables

The user activity log table is an important one from an audit perspective. Other tables, e.g., those that control access to applications, are also sensitive, and auditors also want IAM to record all changes to sensitive data (users, roles, application-to-role access rights, etc.) Each such table should have columns to record the user ID of the user who requested the change, the user ID of the user who authorised the change, as well as timestamps for each of those actions. Since the columns holding these request/authorise fields only pertain to the latest change to a record, we need a way to store the entire history of changes to a table in a reliable way.

Here's a simple mechanism: For every table that needs its change history recorded, create 3 database triggers, one each on the INSERT, UPDATE and DELETE actions. For each table, also create a history table that has all the same fields as the original, but whose primary key is a meaning-free sequence number. This table also needs another special field that says what action resulted in a record being logged. The values of this column would be INS (for inserted record), UPO (for updated old record), UPN (for updated new record) and DEL (for deleted record).

The advantage of database triggers is that changes to tables are logged even if a user bypasses the IAM application and directly updates a table.

The following diagram illustrates how a table's change history can be automatically maintained.

Automated tracking of changes to tables for audit purposes using history tables and database triggers[41]

10/06/2009: Jane Doe joins the organisation, recorded by user 1022

A new record is inserted in the user table

PK	UUID	Name	Updated by	Timestamp
1124	...	Jane Doe	1022	10/06/09 ...

INSERT Trigger →

A record is inserted in the user history table

SeqNo	Type	PK	UUID	Name	Updated by	Timestamp
102	INS	1124	...	Jane Doe	1022	10/06/09 ...

Same fields as in the original table

02/07/2010: Jane marries, changes her name to Jane Smith, recorded by user 1154

The record in the user table is updated

PK	UUID	Name	Updated by	Timestamp
1124	...	Jane Smith	1154	02/07/10 ...

UPDATE Trigger →

Two records are inserted in the user history table

SeqNo	Type	PK	UUID	Name	Updated by	Timestamp
287	UPO	1124	...	Jane Doe	1154	02/07/10 ...
288	UPN	1124	...	Jane Smith	1154	02/07/10 ...

08/10/2011: Jane Smith leaves the organisation, recorded by user 1035

The record in the user table is deleted

PK	UUID	Name	Updated by	Timestamp

DELETE Trigger →

A record is inserted in the user history table

SeqNo	Type	PK	UUID	Name	Updated by	Timestamp
435	DEL	1124	...	Jane Smith	1035	08/10/11 ...

Fig 45: Database triggers for audit history tables

---

[41] Strictly speaking, user records are not usually deleted when a user leaves the organisation, but merely *marked deleted* (i.e., an update). The example above illustrates the generic mechanism which may be useful for other tables.

Rest Easy with REST Services

For a variety of reasons, it's good to maintain a service interface to the functions of IAM. Services are the way to hide the gory details of the implementation from client applications. The traditional approach to building services involves the use of SOAP-based web services. Without getting into the larger SOAP-versus-REST debate, we find that IAM's user management functionality is extremely intuitive and easy to build using REST-based services.

For those unfamiliar with REST, think of it as a way to interact with a web application, with just a few special features. One, although the interaction is over HTTP, the content need not be HTML rendered by a browser. It could be any data structure sent from one application to another. Two, the interaction can be defined quite rigorously, so that the "service contract" so beloved of SOA practitioners is exposed in a recognisable way. Three, although the HTTP protocol appears to be synchronous and also an "unreliable" protocol, it is possible to model asynchronous and reliable behaviour using some standard techniques.

The REST style consists of modelling the various aspects of an application domain as "resources", and dealing with other systems in terms of "representations" of those resources. Representations are somewhat akin to the immutable Data Transfer Objects used in distributed computing.

What makes REST simple is the standardisation of its service interface. There are standard verbs for operations and standard status codes that they return. The resources managed by a server are also exposed in a fairly standard way, i.e., as URIs. In true service-oriented fashion, the actual implementation is completely opaque to the outside world. Only the URIs representing resources, the standard verbs and the standard status codes are ever known by external systems. REST is another great decoupling technique, effectively minimising and formalising the dependencies between service consumers and service providers.

The following diagram helps to understand the REST idiom at a glance.

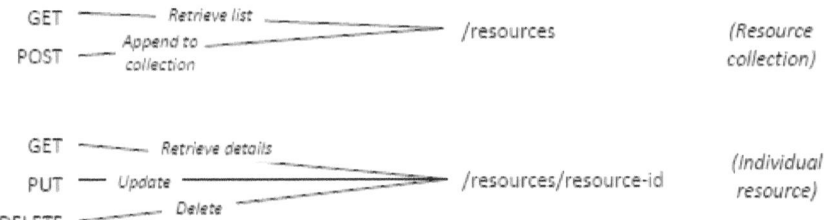

Fig 46: The REST idiom

The design of REST-based services is generally a subtle art, because resources need to be conceptualised in such a way that standard verbs will operate on them in a polymorphic way. Fortunately, IAM functionality is quite intuitive to start with, so the REST service interfaces for IAM pretty much design themselves! Low-ceremony documentation will therefore suffice, and there is no need for the elaborate WSDL and WS-Policy files that are required with SOAP-based services.

The table on the following page illustrates what an IAM REST service interface could look like.

IAM REST Service Interface at a Glance

This is an indicative example. You can design your interface differently, or with more specialised services.

Function	Internal (B2E) Users	B2B Users	B2C Users[42]	Response codes
Create a new user, letting IAM generate the User UUID[43] (User data in request body)	POST /b2eusers/	POST /b2busers/	POST /b2cusers/	201 Created 202 Accepted[44] 400 Bad request
Create a new user using User UUID provided by service consumer (User data in request body)	PUT /b2eusers/{UUID}	PUT /b2busers/{UUID}	PUT /b2cusers/{UUID}	201 Created 202 Accepted, 400 Bad request
Retrieve a user's details	GET /b2eusers/{UUID}	GET /b2busers/{UUID}	GET /b2cusers/{UUID}	200 OK 404 Not found
Retrieve a list or subset of users, with an optional qualifier	GET /b2eusers/?qualification=...	GET /b2busers/?qualification=...	GET /b2cusers/?qualification=...	200 OK 404 Not found
Update a user's attributes (Changed attributes in request body)	PUT (ideally PATCH) /b2eusers/{UUID}	PUT (ideally PATCH) /b2busers/{UUID}	PUT (ideally PATCH) /b2cusers/{UUID}	200 OK 404 Not found 409 Conflict[45]
Delete, deactivate or mark a user record for archival	DELETE /b2eusers/{UUID}	DELETE /b2busers/{UUID}	DELETE /b2cusers/{UUID}	200 OK 404 Not found 410 Gone[46]

Table 2: REST service interface

---

[42] B2B2C users may be supported either through separate URIs, or by reusing the B2C URIs if their treatment is likely to be the same.
[43] On success, the response includes the HTTP header "Location: /{usertype}/{UUID}"
[44] "201 Created" is a synchronous response. "202 Accepted" is an asynchronous acknowledgement, i.e., the request has been successfully received but will be acted on later.
[45] A "409 Conflict" response is used when an attempted update would put the resource into an inconsistent state. "500 Internal service error" is also a possibility in all cases.
[46] "410 Gone" would specifically signify that the record has already been deleted, and is used instead of "404 Not found" as a confirmation of idempotent behaviour.

Automated User Provisioning – Invocation of REST Services

We visualise two groups of "upstream" applications that will invoke the REST services exposed by IAM, in addition to any business applications that may need direct access to user data.

The first is an HR type system, which is the authoritative source for employee onboarding and offboarding. User creation and deletion within IAM may need to be triggered by the corresponding events in this system.

The second is a resource management system that is used to grant and revoke user access to various business applications. User role assignments in IAM may need to be triggered when the corresponding access rights are assigned or deassigned in this system.

An important consideration is the two-phase request/authorise model that follows from the Segregation of Duties principle. You will need to decide whether the request/authorise phases occur in the upstream system (in which case the invocation to IAM is simply to action the decision), or whether both the request and the authorisation need to be communicated to IAM and recorded as two separate events. This has implications on where logging is done, for example.

Model 1 (Request/Authorise steps are performed outside of IAM)

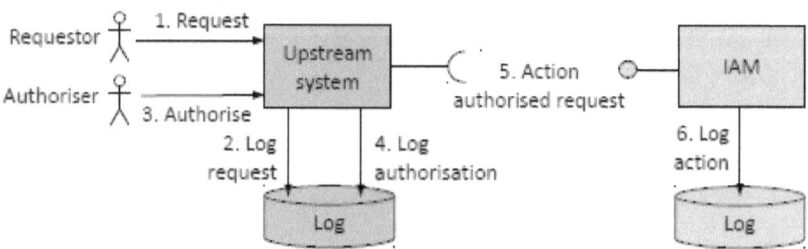

Fig 47: Request/Authorise model 1

Model 2 (Request/Authorise steps are performed through IAM)

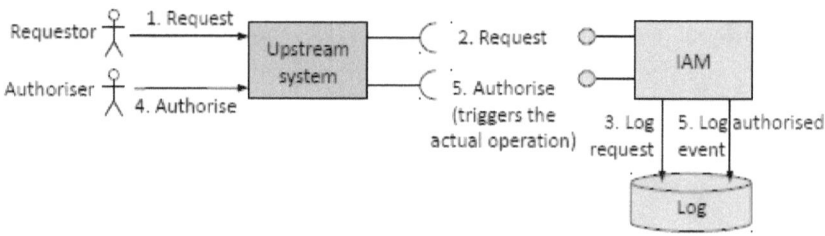

Fig 48: Request/Authorise model 2

Identity Management on a Shoestring

Example – Invocation of REST Services

Here's an indicative overview of how the IAM REST services may be invoked by other systems. GET interfaces are not shown but implied everywhere.

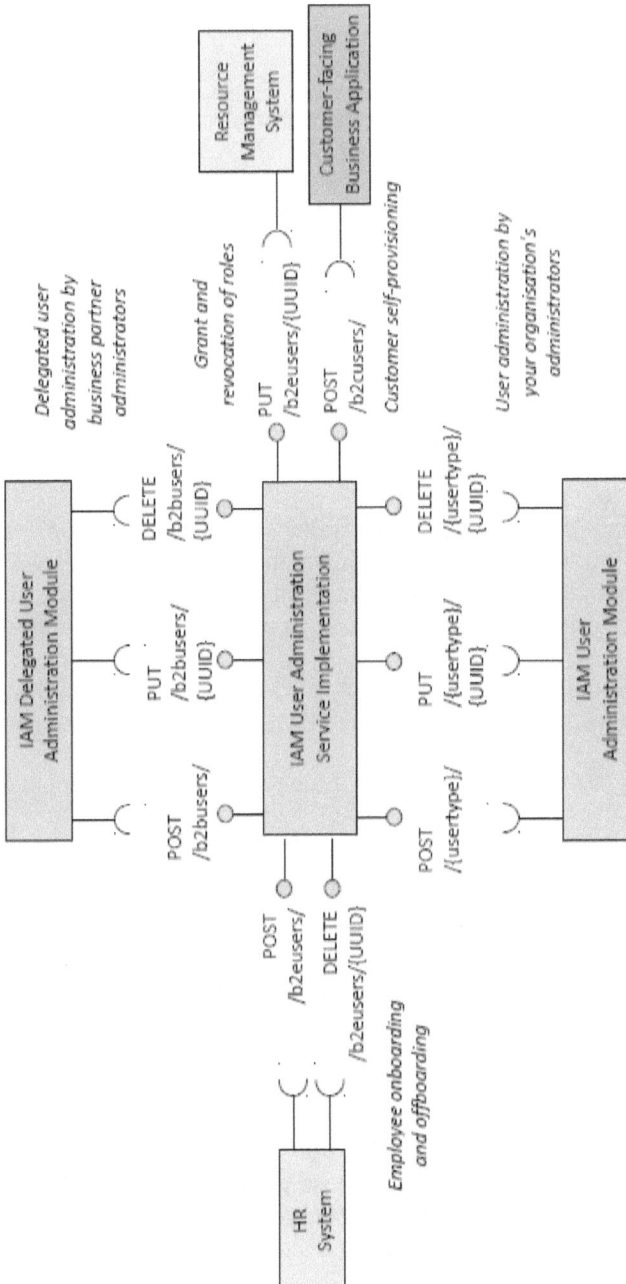

Fig 49: REST service invocation

User Administration

It may seem like wheel reinvention to build an application for user administration when so many vendor IAM products exist to provide this capability out of the box.

Although we started off with similar misgivings, we quickly realised a few things. As we said before, most vendor products are over-designed and tend to cover a much larger set of functionality than your organisation is likely to need. Their processes may not match what your organisation normally does. They may use different (generic) terminology for similar concepts, which could confuse users who are accustomed to the business-specific terms used within the organisation. Aspects like workflow are definite overkill. In short, all of this complexity in an off-the-shelf product requires specialised training, and will continue to mystify newbies to the system in future too. Ironically, these products could miss some specialised functionality that you *do* need.

We also found that a user administration module built using standard web technology is an application of only moderate complexity that is well within the capabilities of an in-house development team to put together fairly quickly. When you use an agile framework like Grails or Roo, you simply define domain objects (based on the data model we presented), and the framework generates the persistence layer and the web interface for you. Customisations to this, such as the two-phase request/authorise process, will be the only real development required.

All this makes IAM User Administration a good candidate for a bespoke application.

If you set out to build a User Administration module, these are the core functions you will need:

User creation:

You'll need to identify the organisations a user belongs to, the user type (B2E, B2B, B2C, etc.), and a few other attributes.

Design this for delegated user administration, so it can be used by your own organisation's administrators as well as by administrators of business partners to manage their own B2B and B2B2C users. Your own administrators get an organisation dropdown to let them choose the set of users they want to look at. Your business partners' administrators only get to see data pertaining to their own organisations. This is easy to implement because IAM protects this application just as it does other business apps, and the logged-in user's organisation should be one of the user attributes passed in.

Design user creation as a two-step process. The user who enters all the details of the user is the "requester". You'll need another screen for an "authoriser" to see all pending user creation requests. It's only after the authoriser authorises a user creation request does the user actually get created and activated. You could create the user record in the IAM database on the creation request but mark it inactive. When authorised, you make it active and also insert the corresponding record in the directory. Needless to say, both steps of the user creation process need to be audit-logged.

Once the user has been created (i.e., on authorisation), send off two separate emails to the user containing their user ID and their password[47]. The password should be pre-expired so that the user has to change it on first login[48].

Other user functions:

User search, View/Edit Selected User and Delete/Deactivate User would be other standard user management functions you will need. Again, design these functions to work in the delegated administration context as well. Deletion should also follow the two-step request/authorise process and be audit-logged at each step.

Protected Applications and Associated Systems:

You will need to define a set of protected applications and associated systems, and provide maintenance screens for these. Protected applications are web applications that need to be hooked into the Access Management side of IAM through interceptors. Associated systems are applications that maintain user data and need to be hooked into the Identity Management side of IAM through user event listeners. A business application could be both a Protected Application and an Associated System, so you may need to provision it as both.

Self-service screens:

Rather than provide these as part of the User Administration module, provide links to "Forgotten ID", "Forgotten Password" and "Reset Security Questions" as part of the CAS login screen.

---

[47] Security folk don't like to see both user ID and password in the same email.
[48] They may also be encouraged or forced to set two or three security questions (E.g., "What is your mother's maiden name?") on their first login to assist with password self-service afterwards. This is an extension to the CAS login screen.

When clicked, the "Forgotten ID" button takes the user to a screen that captures the user's email address. Check the email address against the IAM database but provide no indication as to whether it was found or not, because this could be an important clue to hackers. Respond with a standard message that the user ID has been sent to the appropriate email address in either case. If the email address is valid, retrieve the corresponding user ID (the ID used to log into the SSO environment) and mail it to that address. Log all these events.

When clicked, the "Forgotten Password" button takes the user to a screen that captures their User ID. It then retrieves their security questions and prompts the user for the answers. If the user answers correctly, a new password is generated, stored in the directory as a pre-expired password, then the password is mailed to the user's email address retrieved from the database. The user will not only have to change their password on first login, they could even be forced to set answers to new security questions. To prevent hackers from distinguishing valid User IDs from invalid ones, prompt the user for answers to two random security questions even when the User ID entered is invalid. Provide a standard error message afterwards, so that invalid User IDs and invalid answers to security questions are treated the same way.

"Reset Security Questions" can only be clicked if the user has entered both User ID and password. Authentication proceeds as before, but they are taken to the Security Questions screen where they may select two or more questions and enter their answers. The Security Questions screen can also be set up to appear on a user's first login. The entry of this data can be made mandatory or optional depending on your organisation's security policy. Once they enter this data, they should be redirected back to the original application they were trying to access.

All of these are important security events, so they must be logged as well.

Reset Password and Unlock Account:

While self-service features exist to help users regain access to the system when they forget their User ID or password, you will also need to provide your administrators the ability to force-reset a user's password and mail them a new one. The administrators are also the only ones who can unlock a user's account after it has been locked out because of a number of incorrect login attempts. It's assumed that they will have already verified the user's bona fides out of band before unlocking the account.

Fine-grained authorisation:

In the LIMA model, we delegate fine-grained authorisation to the respective business applications themselves because these rules are best defined close to where they are used. The rate of change of such detailed information also militates against their management at an enterprise level.

However, we do have some options to make an administrator's life easier.

We can loosely couple the administration screens of IAM and the business applications, so that when the administrator is finished creating a user on IAM, they can follow a hyperlink to the business application's own user administration screen and continue the fine-grained provisioning from there. Since the business application is protected by IAM's SSO regime, and since the administrator has a suitable role within the application that gives them access to this screen, the navigation will be seamless, uninterrupted by any login screen or other access challenge. There may be a change in the look-and-feel of the two applications, but this is cosmetic rather than functional.

To be truly loosely-coupled, each user must store their own browser bookmarks to the different user provisioning screens, but to sweeten the pill of having to cross application boundaries to perform this function, it may be desired to provide hyperlinks to the business applications' user admin screens from within the IAM user admin screen. Since it's not expected that the URIs of these admin screens will change frequently, it may not be a bad compromise.

Role Type, Application-Role and User-Application-Role associations:

Arguably the most important part of user administration is the grant and revocation of access rights to applications. Keeping in mind that IAM only manages coarse-grained authorisation, you will need screens to define generic enterprise roles, associations between generic roles and applications to create application-specific roles (coarse-grained, of course), and finally the mapping of users to these application-specific roles.

All grants and revocations should be two-phase (request/authorise), and they must be logged.

Reports:

Every organisation needs a unique and different set of user reports, so it would be pointless to try and list them out. We can talk about categories of reports to consider, though.

Some of these would be audit reports, and they could be exception-based. Other reports could be daily and periodic statistics (e.g., number of new users provisioned, etc.) Yet other reports could be reconciliation reports, to ensure that user data on various different systems are consistent.

For Java-based web applications, BIRT is an excellent report-generation tool.

IAM, Protect Thyself

One of the interesting side-effects of building an IAM system using web technology (especially the user administration screens and REST services) is that it can be elegantly secured using its own authentication and authorisation mechanism. No special measures are necessary.

Tip 1: Define a role called "Administrator" under an application called "IAM" in the database, and associate specific users with this application role

With this, an interceptor sitting in front of the IAM Administration module will work exactly the same way as interceptors that sit in front of business applications (i.e., by restricting access to this application to only authorised administrators).

Tip 2: Build security for REST services in the same manner as for a web app

The same principle holds true for the REST services. Since these are HTTP calls, they can also be intercepted in exactly the same way as requests for web pages. Applications that invoke REST services will need to use HTTP Basic Authentication and send their system account names and passwords as part of the service call (over SSL, of course). IAM will authenticate these credentials against its directory just as it does for human users. There are standard ways to encrypt and store system account passwords on the respective application servers such that they are not accessible or usable by developers or other staff who happen to have access to the servers. Consult your system administrators to implement these measures.

Tip 3: Build support for delegated user administration using exactly the same code base as for regular user administration

CAS can retrieve any required user attributes from the database and pass them into an application. The organisation that a user belongs to can be one of these attributes. The IAM administration module can implement a level of fine-grained access control by modifying the content of user management screens based on the organisation that the logged-in user belongs to.

If the logged-in user belongs to your own organisation, you can assume that they are your own administrators and are to be given access to user management functions across your organisation as well as those of business partners. User management screens can have dropdowns allowing the user to select an organisation before performing user administration functions. This is standard user administration.

If the logged-in user belongs to a partner organisation, they should only get to see information pertaining to their own organisation. They cannot select an organisation from a dropdown because they are sandboxed within their own organisational context. This is delegated user administration.

Tip 4: Tailor the appearance of the delegated administration module to the partner organisation

The look-and-feel of the administration module can be tailored to conform to the style of the partner organisation's website, because the logged-in user's organisation is one of the attributes that is passed into the application. You only need to hold stylesheets on your website with appropriate naming conventions, and use codes for partner organisations that can be substituted into a template to get the appropriate stylesheet name.

Using some very simple techniques, you can produce a fairly sophisticated and flexible user administration module for both internal and external administrators, and also secure it effectively.

Provisioning Users to Downstream Systems

The standards body OASIS has a comprehensive model for user provisioning that is shown in Appendix B. They also specify a markup language to be used for user provisioning, called SPML (Service Provisioning Markup Language). Although SPML seems very rigorous and promising, the entire SPML standard is just a shell that defines the schema of the XML message envelope. The actual message body is left to the discretion of the implementing organisation.

SPML also assumes a request/response model that may be too constraining. We have found value in treating the semantics of user provisioning as a simple event broadcast rather than as a request/response interaction between systems. IAM should not have to "know" what downstream systems exist, for the purpose of provisioning to them. That would be a form of tight coupling. The list of downstream systems should be maintained in a flexible and dynamic way, because IAM is rolled out to application after application over a period of time, and this needs to be done without much incremental effort, which includes changes to IAM. A loosely-coupled interaction model would therefore be more robust and operationally cost-effective in a real-world organisational environment. Here, IAM would only need to "announce" an event, and it would be up to all concerned downstream systems to act on it.

Therefore, after a lot of deliberation, we concluded that standards-compliance for its own sake wasn't worth the cost in complexity and that a simpler scheme was desirable.

Tip 1: Use a Publish/Subscribe model to propagate user events to systems "downstream" of IAM

Multiple systems that maintain local copies of user data need to be notified when there are changes to user data (adds, updates and deletes). They only need to register with IAM to receive such notifications. Such a publish/subscribe model is easily implemented through a "bus" mechanism. IAM publishes user events on this bus and systems subscribing to these events receive such messages and make updates to their local data accordingly. This is the "User Event Bus".

Tip 2: The User Event Bus must deliver messages to listeners in a secure and reliable way

The User Event Bus has certain required characteristics:

- Secure subscription model: A system may register an interest in user events by subscribing to them. Systems must be validated at the time they subscribe using an authentication scheme that is supported by the queue or broker product used. This prevents unauthorised systems and applications from tapping into the bus to listen on user provisioning messages. The bus may additionally encrypt messages to prevent eavesdropping by third parties.

- Persistent messages: User provisioning messages are crucial for downstream systems and cannot afford to be lost, otherwise the loss of synchronisation will lead to many application errors or even security breaches. Hence messages must be persisted so that they can be recovered even if the bus crashes.

- Durable subscriptions: Given a large enough ecosystem, some system or the other is bound to be offline at any given time. User provisioning messages must eventually be delivered to all of them even if they were offline at the time the event occurred. The bus must therefore store messages that should be delivered to a system until it comes back online.

- Guarantee of delivery: When an administrator makes a change to user data, or when an upstream system makes a REST service call into IAM making such a change, they need an immediate acknowledgement that the message will eventually be delivered. It is not feasible to provide a real-time acknowledgement that the message has been acted upon by all downstream systems because this is not a synchronous process.

Tip 3: Manage by exception, and avoid notification of the status of processing if at all possible

Given the guarantee of eventual delivery, it is sufficient for a downstream system to quietly process the event. Silence signifies successful processing, just like in the Unix environment.

Tip 4: Where notification is unavoidable, use a simple acknowledgement event on the same bus

In rare cases, a user event may require a response. An example is when a new user is to be provisioned on a mainframe, but (1) IAM cannot authoritatively generate the user ID on the mainframe, and (2) the mainframe cannot store a reference to the User UUID locally. The mainframe has to generate an appropriate user ID, then notify IAM of this user ID so that IAM can update its "User-Associated System" table. In such cases, the downstream system's event listener must place an acknowledgement message on the bus, which IAM subscribes to.

This model is illustrated below:

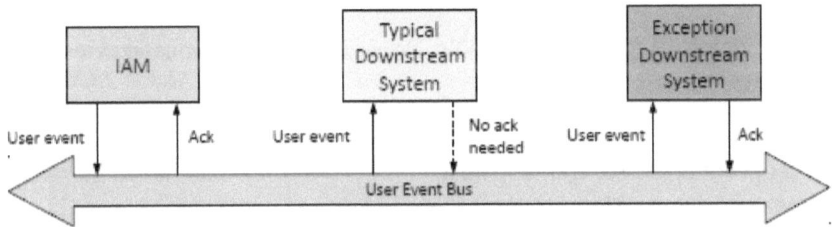

Fig 50: User event bus

Tip 5: Separate error-handling out into a different mechanism and don't overload the User Event Bus with error messages

We have noticed that in most cases, errors in processing user events are because of (transient) problems in the local system and not because of errors in the actual message. In rare cases, they may be because of errors in systems upstream of IAM, such as the HR system. It is simplest for such processing errors to be recorded and reported on locally. The administrators of downstream systems are usually best placed to understand why processing failed and to fix it.

Handle these errors using a separate mechanism altogether rather than clutter the User Event Bus with error messages. Define a suitable error message format (Error UUID, User Event UUID, Status Code, Description, Timestamp, Original Message, etc.)

All listeners should log errors to a separate error queue. An administration interface to this queue should be able to provide alerts and reports as well as a query view into the contents of the queue. Sending such error messages back to IAM is usually not of much use, although in practice, the same users who administer the IAM module may also monitor the error queue. In any case, it's not a good idea to tightly couple these two roles through the design. Better keep error-handling logically separate from the user administration function, and grant a user access to both functions if required.

Tip 6: Don't design the user provisioning model as a distributed transaction

The failure of any one downstream system to process a user event does not mean that the change must be rolled back on all other systems. Such a requirement not only makes this system overly complex and tightly-coupled, it is also not warranted.

Designing User Provisioning Messages

The basic idea is to keep things simple. Provisioning-related messages are of the following types:

1. User events (that IAM publishes to associated systems)
2. User event acknowledgements (used only when some data has to be returned from associated systems to IAM)
3. User event processing errors (to be handled separately)

The actual format of data is up to the preference of an individual organisation. Some prefer XML, while others may choose JSON. We're agnostic about this level of design detail, because it's more important to get the higher level right. At this higher level, there are perhaps two major message data models that can be used to transport user events.

1. Ideal Model (exploiting the User UUID and the property of idempotence):

In the ideal case, all downstream systems understand the User UUID as a candidate key for a user within their own data stores. This facilitates a very simple model of user event propagation.

On any user event that occurs within IAM (i.e., user creation, user deletion, change of user attributes, provisioning or de-provisioning on an associated system), a simple snapshot of the user's profile is all that needs to be broadcast on the User Event Bus. Here's what this looks like:

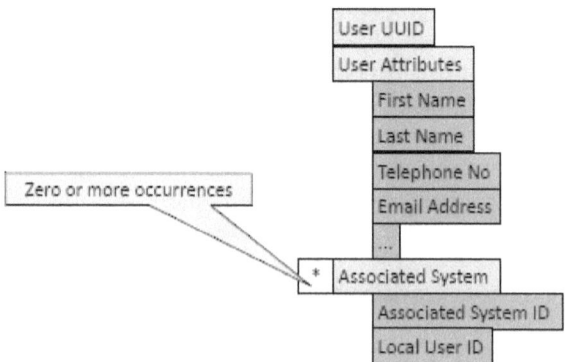

Fig 51: Simple user event

There are only three top-level elements of this message – the User UUID, a composite "User Attributes" element comprised of individual elements (e.g., first name, last name), and an optional repeating element called "Associated System", which contains the ID of each associated system where that user's data is to be held, along with the local User ID of the user within that system.

The semantics of such a message are simple.

If an associated system is referenced in the message through its ID, then the requirement is for that system to "create or update" the user and to record whichever user attributes are required by that system. This message can even be used to modify the Local User ID on a system.

If an associated system is not referenced anywhere in the message, then the requirement is for that system to "delete or ignore" the user. If the user is currently held in the system, the record is to be deleted (or marked deleted). If the user is not currently held in the system, the message is to be ignored.

The idempotence property ensures that repeated receipt of a message by a system will have no additional effect after the first one.

This is therefore the simplest user provisioning model, and the one we recommend.

The only complication here is with systems that need to generate their own Local User ID and cannot accept one supplied by IAM. In such cases, IAM would simply leave the Local User ID field blank. The associated system will generate this ID, then send back a User Event Acknowledgement message with the mapping of this ID to the User UUID, so that IAM can update its "User-Associated System" table.

The User Event Acknowledgement message may look like this:

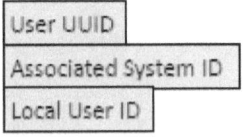

Fig 52: User event ack

Needless to say, if there is even one system that has to generate its own Local User IDs, IAM would have to be configured to listen on User Event Acknowledgement messages. As always, messages are assumed to be persistent and IAM's subscription to these messages is assumed to be durable, so no messages will be lost even in the event of a bus crash or IAM being temporarily offline.

2. Fallback Model (when the User UUID is not universally supported):

If the User UUID cannot be relied upon to be a candidate key across systems, then the user provisioning data design expectedly becomes less elegant and more complex. The Local User ID now has to be relied on as the only identifying "key" on systems that do not support the User UUID.

We find that instead of sending out a single, standard representation of current user state, we will need to send four different messages based on the nature of the user event. These are:

1. Create User
2. Delete User
3. Update User Attributes
4. Change Local User ID

The "Create User" message would look like this:

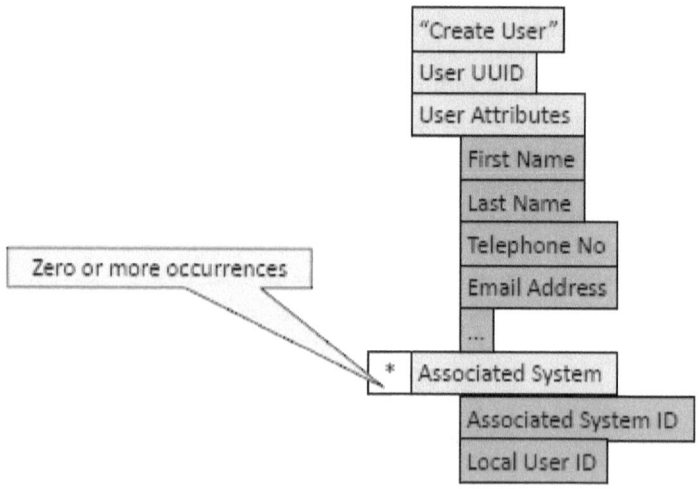

Fig 53: Create User message

This looks just like the standard snapshot message of the ideal model, but with the "Create User" verb explicitly specified. The implicit "create or update" and "delete or ignore" semantics are no longer possible to assume, because the Local User ID is now the only key for some systems, and it may not be possible for IAM to specify it in case it has to be locally generated.

— When the user already exists and is to be provisioned on an additional associated system, only that associated system's data need be included in the "Associated System" attribute. Existing systems need not be referenced in the message. Only that system will then create the user record, and other systems will ignore it.

— When the associated system needs to generate the Local User ID, the Local User ID field may need to carry a special value such as "LOCALLY_GENERATED".

The "Delete User" message would look like this:

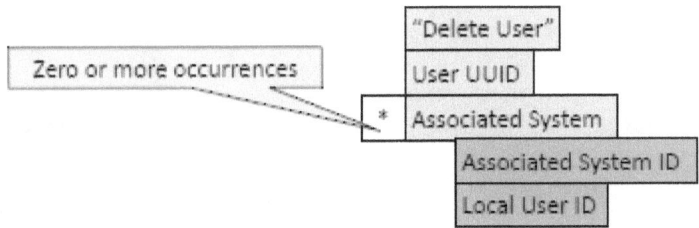

Fig 54: Delete User message

- The Local User ID attribute need only be provided for those systems that don't support the User UUID. Those that do can delete (or mark deleted) a user based on the User UUID.

- When using this message to revoke user provisioning from just a few associated systems, the Associated System section should only contain their IDs. Other associated systems that are not referenced will ignore this message.

The "Update User Attributes" message would resemble the "Create User" message but with the verb "Update User Attributes" instead. Only those systems that don't support the User UUID need to be referenced in the Associated Systems section. Every associated system would be able to update user attributes based on the candidate key it understands (User UUID or Local User ID).

A special "Change Local User ID" message is now required because for some systems, there is only one candidate key, so updating the value of that key is no longer straightforward. This is what this message would look like:

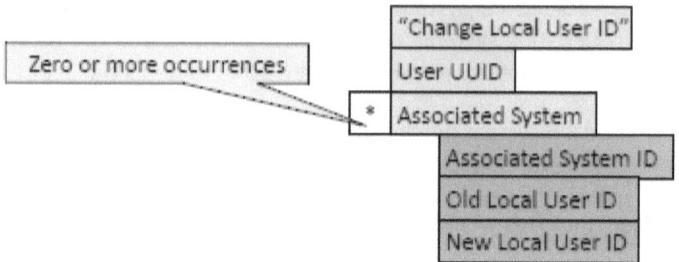

Fig 55: Change local user ID message

As you can see, life gets more complicated when the User UUID is not universally supported. It may be worth maintaining a "User UUID-to-Local User ID" mapping behind an associated system's User Event Listener, so that it appears as if the associated system itself understands the User UUID.

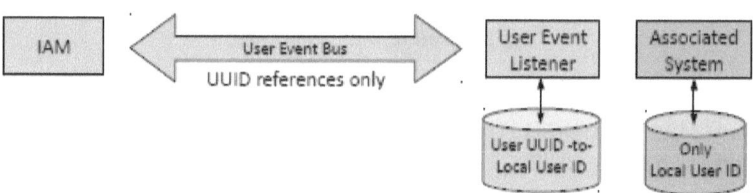

Fig 56: User Event listener

Implementing LIMA

The previous sections have given you an idea of what the design of a loosely-coupled IAM system could look like. However, there are also many logistical aspects to consider when rolling out such a system, because implementation comes with its own pitfalls. Finally, even when the IAM system is in "steady state" with no new functionality enhancements required, there are still some standard tasks to be performed every time a new application is to be brought within its ambit. This section looks at all of these aspects.

Transitioning to the Target State

You need to plan the development of IAM functionality based on the requirements of business projects, and take advantage of project budgets to fund their development. Appendix E shows how you could align the IAM roadmap to the requirements of business projects to achieve viability through incremental funding.

There are some specific items you need to pay attention to during this process.

Harmonising data

You will start with data held redundantly in multiple systems, with inconsistencies and errors galore. You plan to end with a reasonably consistent set of user data, with one or more directories holding authentication credentials, and a user database holding other user attributes. Upstream sources of truth will populate and refresh these repositories. Downstream replicas of data will be refreshed through IAM-generated user events.

Partway along this journey, you will have problems harmonising the data you have painstakingly marshalled into the IAM repositories with data that is outside its ambit. There will be people and systems furiously updating what should rightly be read-only replicas. Upstream sources of truth will have no way to communicate changes reliably and consistently to the IAM system. You will need to create mitigating controls, manual processes and temporary applications and scripts to maintain a semblance of sanity.

As you progress towards the IAM vision, remember that the User UUID is your friend. If you can push the UUID vision and gain buy-in from owners of systems, you can start seeding those independent repositories with the data hooks that you can later use to "reel in" those disparate user records. The good news is that lots of people can appreciate the value of the UUID when it is explained to them, and many systems, databases and directories can support a UUID field.

Managing SSO realms

It may happen that you have rolled IAM out to an intranet application but have not exploited SPNEGO or Active Directory integration, perhaps because there were too many changes being introduced and you didn't want to overly complicate things at that stage. The user provisioning is therefore applied to the IAM directory (not Active Directory) and database. Next, you plan to roll out IAM to another intranet application, this time exploiting SPNEGO and Active Directory. Let's say there's an overlap between the two sets of users, so there are some users who will need to access both these applications. Let's also say that the LAN user ID for these users is different from their SSO user ID as stored in the IAM directory[49]. How will you proceed?

Well, it depends on whether you want these users to have Single Sign-On across these two applications right away, or whether you would like to keep the logins separate for a while and provide Single Sign-On only after you "harmonise" the User ID scheme.

If you want these users to get Single Sign-On rightaway, then you must ensure that this intersecting group of users has the same UUID within AD and in the IAM directory. Since both applications use CAS, the first application they hit will result in a Ticket-Granting Ticket being generated and stored in a browser cookie against the CAS server's domain name. The TGT will also be stored in the ticket registry with that user's UUID in the BLOB attribute. When the user then tries to access the second application (no matter in which order the two are accessed), the browser will present the TGT to CAS and CAS will dutifully refrain from challenging them afresh for their authentication credentials. But here's the rub. The information about the user that's associated with the TGT in the Service Registry has been retrieved from the database based on the UUID stored in the directory. Unless the UUIDs of the user in the two directories are the same, the user information could be different depending on the order in which the applications are accessed. This is why users who need to access multiple applications need to have a consistent UUID across the user repositories they span.

If, on the other hand, you're content to delay Single Sign-On until all user authentication data is consistently and non-redundantly stored in one or the other directory, you will need to maintain two CAS domain names, because CAS will need to create two TGT cookies, and the only way to do that without conflict is to store them under two different domain names. You may use domain names like "sso.myorg.com" and "sso-spnego.myorg.com", for example. That way, when the user tries to access the second application, there will be no TGT cookie corresponding to that CAS domain, so CAS will challenge the user or browser for their credentials afresh. This is acceptable as long as the users understand that they will enter their IAM SSO credentials when trying to access the first application. The second application will silently use their LAN credentials.

---

[49] E.g., LAN user IDs could be 6-character strings, while SSO User IDs could have a "firstname.lastname" scheme.

Manual provisioning

User provisioning is a function that is typically carried out by a back-end Security Operations department. The demand for automation of user provisioning typically comes from those managing this function as a cost centre. Business projects and business units typically don't care about this because the effort is transparent to them. So automated user provisioning is one of those IAM features that you may find hard to get funded through project budgets, and the development here may only inch forward unless you secure some enterprise funding to help out.

The moral of the story is that while new applications will keep coming under the IAM umbrella from an Access Management perspective (the most visible and sensitive aspect for auditors), the back-end Identity Management side will usually lag behind quite badly. You may go for long periods with an increased manual provisioning load while you cope with the larger number of users being managed by IAM.

Keep the user provisioning screens as easy to use as possible, so the burden on the administrators is lessened. And keep lobbying with the powers-that-be for increased funding for automated user provisioning. Fortunately, the headcount savings through automation are tangible, so a business case for this can eventually be made.

Identity Management on a Shoestring

The BAU of IAM – A "Cookie-Cutter" Implementation

You've almost arrived. You have implemented every feature of IAM your organisation needs, but there are still some applications out there that need to be brought under the umbrella of IAM. How easily can you mop them up? Well, while IAM integration at this stage is still not a no-cost operation, it's almost certainly a "known cost" one.

Here are some of the things you typically need to do:

Development tasks

1. Implement a CAS interceptor for the application using an appropriate technology[50]. Disable the application's native authentication mechanism. Modify it to operate in a trusted mode and accept user attributes passed into it by the interceptor instead.

2. Disable local user management functions (the parts dealing with user creation, deletion and the update of common user attributes) and only retain the fine-grained role mapping and access control rules specific to the application.

3. Implement a listener to provision and de-provision users, and to update common user attributes in an automated fashion based on user events received over the User Event Bus.

4. If required, create a hyperlink on the IAM administration module to enable an administrator to jump to this application's fine-grained role mapping screen as soon as a user is provisioned through IAM[51].

---

[50] Some examples of interceptors for CAS are a CAS servlet filter, a container mechanism like WebSphere's Trust Association Interceptor, the Apache web server's mod_auth_cas module, Spring security or a global authenticating reverse proxy.

[51] Although the user event from IAM is propagated to the application's event listener through a store-and-forward mechanism (i.e., the User Event Bus), in practice, this happens extremely fast and the user would most probably have been created within the application by the time the administrator clicks on the link and opens the application's fine-grained role assignment screen. IAM's SSO ensures that the hyperlink navigation will be seamless and the administrator will not have to log into the application.

Provisioning tasks

1. Prepare a mail in advance of the actual roll-out informing users of the cutover date and their new user IDs (if required) after that date.

2. Based on the list of current application users drawn from its user database, run batch scripts to do the following:

   a) Assign UUIDs to these users

   b) If login user IDs need to change to conform to an enterprise standard or convention, apply these new user IDs.

   c) Either batch-load the UUIDs into the application (if it can hold such references) or batch-load the UUID-application user ID mapping into IAM's Associated System table.

   d) On the cutover day (or night), run a batch script to insert user records into the IAM directory and database. The batch script will generate random passwords and create them in the directory as expired passwords. This will force the user to change their password on first login.

   e) Send out two emails to each user, one with the application's URL and the new user ID, and a separate one with their password. Inform them that they will need to set their password on first login, and it will need to conform to the organisation's password policy.

These are the same operations you would perform each time a new application is to be "onboarded" to the IAM ecosystem. They are fairly standard (although each application will require special tweaks) and are consequently easy to estimate. The costs are likely to be low enough to justify funding from a project bucket rather than require enterprise intervention.

With each such roll-out, you would be taking your organisation a step closer to its IAM nirvana.

Conclusion

We have covered the design of an Identity and Access Management system in fairly great detail in this paper.

The core philosophy of the LIMA approach is loose coupling between the various functional components of IAM. In most cases, the loose coupling is from the use of appropriate data design, specifically a meaning-free identifier. Other elements of loose coupling are replicated data using master data management principles, event notification and idempotent messages.

We have also provided tips to aid the design of the user data stores, user administration functions and a simple service interface.

The LIMA approach obviates the need for expensive and complex commercial IAM products, yet avoids reinventing the wheel (especially for security-sensitive processes) by leveraging commodity components like CAS and Shibboleth for access management. It also allows you to design the bespoke parts of an IAM system based on some simple foundations and extend it as required using technologies and tools familiar to your organisation.

In spite of its simplicity, the LIMA approach adheres to security principles (as enunciated in an early section), so it is not a naïve oversimplification of IAM.

We have not spelt out the many wrong turns we took in our own implementation, but rest assured there were many. We have told you only the successful design decisions we finally arrived at, and also the decisions that we know we should have made, even if we didn't. So this document contains many hundreds of thousands of dollars worth of hard experience, corresponding to the amount of money you will save compared to either a proprietary commercial IAM product roll-out or a completely independent in-house development with its inevitable missteps and suboptimal choices. Of course, you may also discover some simplifications and optimisations of your own, so this document is by no means the last word on IAM. In any case, we hope our experience as documented here will illuminate your path and make your IAM implementation even more successful than ours. (Don't forget to have an independent security audit done of your system before you go live!)

Good luck, and good hunting!

Appendix A – Typical Security Requirements from an IAM System

Security/audit staff tend to expect certain core features in an IAM system, as listed below. While the LIMA approach supports them, you must ensure that your design actually meets them.

Access Management		
	Requirement	How the LIMA design supports it
1	Each user of the system must have a unique ID. This cannot be shared between users. A user must be defined only once on a system.	The design features unique login IDs for users as well as unique IDs (UUIDs) for users across systems.
2	Except for systems allowing anonymous access, any access to a system must only be granted when a user supplies their ID and a password. For some systems, an additional token (two-factor authentication) may be required.	Authentication is mandatory with interceptors that force the validation of user credentials. Different types of identity assertions are supported. Two-factor authentication is a simple extension.
3	User IDs used for logging into applications must have expiry dates and an active/disabled flag.	User records in the IAM database have a creation date, an effective (start) date and an expiry date. The LDAP directory supports an active/inactive user attribute.
4	Passwords must be stored securely using one-way encryption (i.e., passwords cannot be reverse-engineered).	The LDAP directory supports standard hashing and encryption algorithms.
5	Passwords must not be displayed in cleartext when entered on a screen.	Special password fields should be used to hide the actual characters being entered.
6	Passwords must have certain characteristics[52].	The LDAP directory supports the specification of password characteristics through policy settings.
7	A User ID and password must never be sent together in the same email or document.	The design of the provisioning system envisages sending user IDs and passwords in separate emails.
8	Role-based access control must be applied when users access business functions and data.	Coarse-grained role-based access control is supported. Fine-grained access control is assumed to be applied by the business application based on user attributes supplied by IAM.
9	Accounts must be locked out after a defined number of failed login attempts.	This is supported by LDAP as a password policy configuration setting.
10	Locked-out accounts are not automatically reactivated and can only be reset by an administrator.	This is supported by LDAP as a password policy configuration setting.

[52] Table 3: Access Management Requirements

---

[52] Examples of password characteristics are minimum length, combinations of alphanumeric, numeric and special characters, expiry period, uniqueness history, change on first login or reset, etc.

	Identity Management	
	Requirement	How the LIMA design supports it
1	Information held about a user should include the following attributes *(as specified)*	The IAM database can be designed to hold whatever attributes are deemed necessary.
2	The user administration function should be logically separate from any business application.	The IAM design envisages a separate user administration web application and an independent set of services.
3	Administrators should have the ability to create or delete users and maintain their access privileges to various systems.	The IAM user administration module would have these features.
4	Access rights must be granted on a least privilege basis. No user must have more access than their job requires.	Control over the scope of access rights is outside the purview of IAM but IAM will not impede the implementation of such policies.
5	There must be segregation of duties relating to user provisioning – an administrator cannot authorise the creation of a user that they have themselves entered.	Two-step processes for all sensitive operations can be supported by the database as well as the user administration application.
6	The system must provide audit and logging capability.	Audit tables can be set up to log all relevant user activity and changes to sensitive tables.
7	Only the system should be able to write to log files/tables.	Database accesses can be set up to ensure this.
8	Log files/tables should only be readable after login or an approved access process.	Database accesses can be set up to ensure this.
9	Audit logs must be retained for a defined period of time and only appended to, never overwritten.	A separate database area for audit makes it possible to manage growth and archival.

Table 4: Identity Management Requirements

Appendix B – Mapping the LIMA Design to the OASIS Model of IAM

OASIS defines Access Management and Identity Management functions using abstract terminology for various components. This is how the OASIS model maps to the LIMA design.

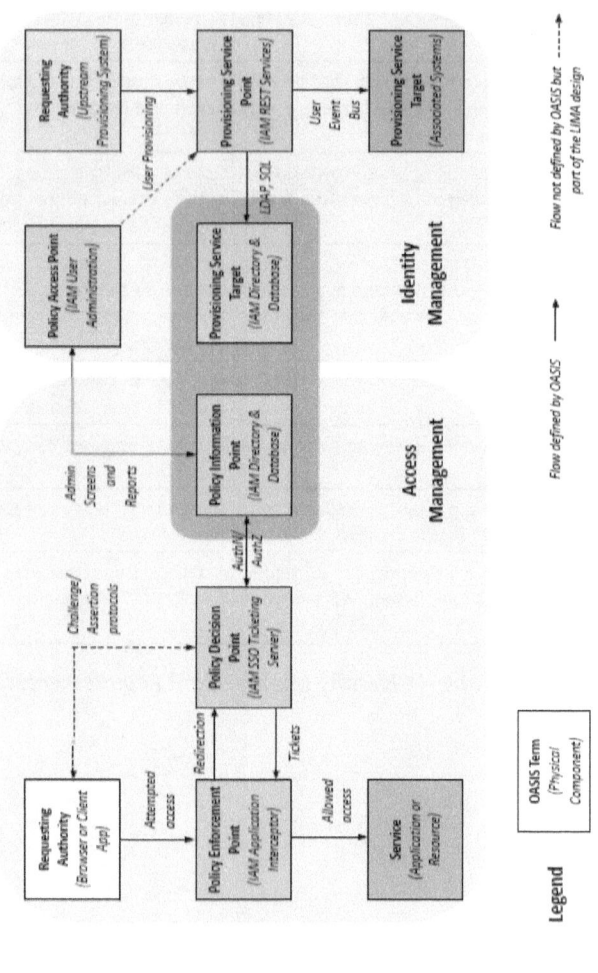

Fig 57: Mapping LIMA to the OASIS model

Identity Management on a Shoestring

Appendix C – Special Case Example 1 (Multiplexing User IDs)

Here is a problem that not every organisation would face, hence it is unlikely to be addressed out-of-the-box by any commercial IAM product. The bespoke solution (multiplexing) is interesting and may be more widely applicable.

Let's say your organisation has a product system running on an old mainframe. You are now required to open up the functionality of this system to the web, to be accessed by B2C users (customers) through a pass-through web application. (Notice that in LIMA terminology, the pass-through web application is your protected application, while your mainframe is your associated system. The mainframe is not directly exposed.)

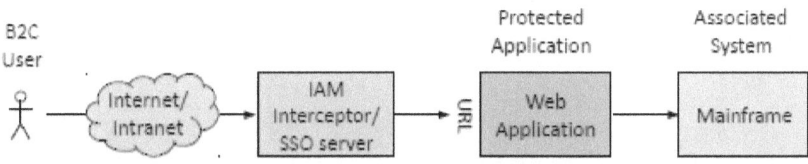

Fig 58: Multiplexing User IDs

Your auditors demand that the activities of each individual customer be tracked as they transact on this sensitive product system. However, the mainframe-based system was never designed to deal with the hundreds of thousands of online customers that are expected. It has severe restrictions on the number of User IDs it can support, perhaps because the User ID field only supports 4 numeric digits. It would cost too much to re-engineer this legacy system to support a much larger number of users. What do you do?

One approach is to think about the number of concurrent users that are expected to access the system. Perhaps this would be in the range of a few thousand, compared to the hundreds of thousands of customers overall. The solution then is to just provision this smaller number of users on the mainframe, and record these as "temporary User IDs" within IAM, to be treated as "access tokens" to the mainframe, handed out to B2C users as they pass through the IAM gauntlet. When users complete their session or log out (however you may define "logout" in a Single Sign-On environment), you release these temporary User IDs back into the "pool" to be reissued to other B2C users. Keep track of which user was granted which access token, and the timestamps between when they held the token, by recording these in a User ID allocation log table. The mainframe only logs the activities of the "temporary User IDs" that it sees. You need to reconcile these IDs with the actual User IDs (UUIDs) that identify physical users, by consulting the User ID allocation log table.

There's a complication, though. Timestamps on IAM and the mainframe may differ, so you may fail to authoritatively establish that it was User A who executed a certain transaction and not the next user, User B. You can sidestep it by passing both the UUID and the temporary User ID to the mainframe through an intermediary integration component, which can log each business transaction request into a transaction log table. This would be a more authoritative way to establish the identity of the physical user who performed a particular transaction on the mainframe.

The following diagram illustrates different ways to map user identity, to enable the tracking of user activity to the satisfaction of your auditors.

Identity Management on a Shoestring

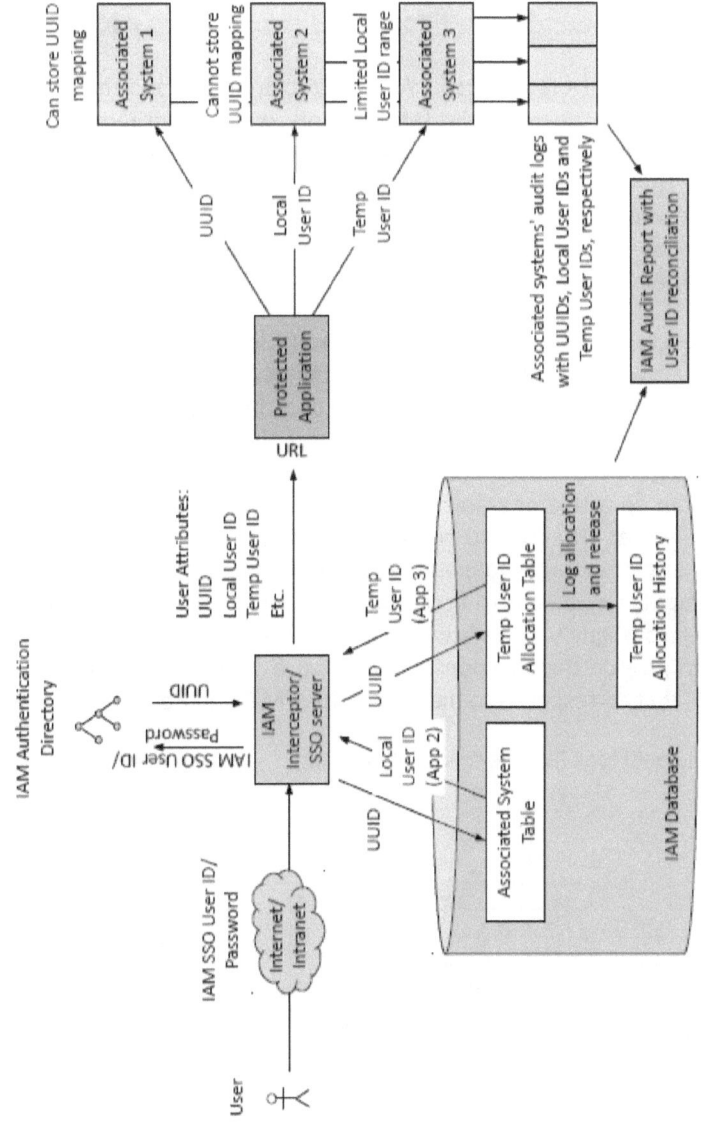

Fig 59: User activity tracking

Appendix D – Special Case Example 2 (Resetting LAN Passwords)

We talked about your organisation's Active Directory setup and the desirability of letting it coexist with the minimalist IAM directory, with neither replacing the other. That approach solves the access management and provisioning problems, but a requirement to support self-service password resets in the Windows LAN environment could also arise. Self-service is important for password resets because the predominant SOS call that hits a corporate helpdesk is a password reset request, and helpdesks are expensive to run.

There are several native Windows products available in the market to do this, but they aren't universally applicable. Remote users who log in through a mechanism like Citrix, for example, may be unable to use such products. The simplest solution would be a web-based application that challenges the user with an alternate set of credentials (e.g., the personal security questions they have previously specified), then sets them up with a one-time password on Active Directory and displays it to them on the screen. They would be forced to change this on their next LAN login. There are many advantages to a web-based application, mainly that the user can use any computer or device to access it and reset their password, most often a neighbouring colleague's workstation. Clearly, there are IAM components that can be reused to provide this functionality, and Active Directory only needs to hold a UUID (GUID) that corresponds to the user in the IAM database.

The solution could look like the following diagram.

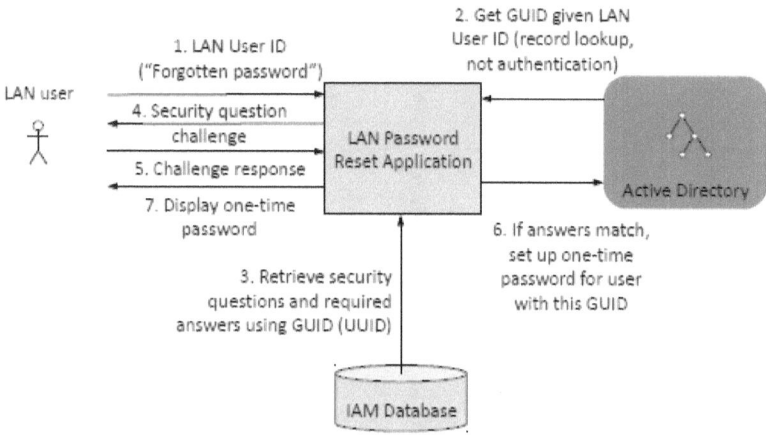

Fig 60: Resetting LAN passwords

Of course, all password reset requests are sensitive from an audit/security perspective, so they should be logged and monitored.

This is another example of how decoupling user identity with a UUID/GUID makes it really simple to integrate components and develop inexpensive solutions to potentially tricky problems. Commercial off-the-shelf solutions tend to be more expensive and yet have limitations that a bespoke solution based on a loosely-coupled architecture does not suffer from.

Appendix E – A Sample Phased Roll-out Plan

Here's a sample plan for rolling out IAM piecemeal using multiple business projects as funding vehicles:

Timeframe	Project/phase	New assets created	Prior assets leveraged
Q1Y1	B2C application	Local interceptor Authentication directory User database External-facing CAS servers REST services (B2C) User self-service screens	N/A
Q3Y1	Partner application 1	Local interceptor and listener User admin screens (including delegated admin) REST services (B2B) User Event Bus	Authentication directory User database External-facing CAS servers
Q1Y2	Intranet application	Local interceptor and listener Internal-facing CAS servers SPNEGO enhancement to CAS REST services (Internal)	Authentication directory User database User Event Bus
Q3Y2	Partner application 2 (employing federated identity)	Local interceptor SAML2 enhancement to CAS	External-facing CAS servers
Q1Y3	New HR system roll-out	REST service calls from HR	REST services (Internal)
...	...	...	...
	Any subsequent system	Local interceptor and listener	All of the above

Table 5: Sample phased rollout plan

About the Authors

Ganesh Prasad (g.c.prasad@gmail.com) has been an architect in the Shared Services space for many years and has convinced himself that his brand of pedantry is in fact a long-term and enterprise-wide perspective. He provides nuisance value to project teams that just want to get the job done.

Umesh Rajbhandari (u.rajbhandari@gmail.com) is a Java / Web developer who likes to keep abreast of the latest technologies. He has worked in Singapore and Nepal, and is currently based in Sydney.

www.ingramcontent.com/pod-product-compliance
Lightning Source LLC
Chambersburg PA
CBHW021951170526
45157CB00003B/941